200 Light
cakes & desserts

hamlyn | **all colour cookbook**

200 Light
cakes & desserts

641.5635

An Hachette UK Company
www.hachette.co.uk

First published in Great Britain in 2015 by Hamlyn
a division of Octopus Publishing Group Ltd, Endeavour
House, 189 Shaftesbury Avenue, London, WC2H 8JY
www.octopusbooks.co.uk

ISBN 13: 978-0-600-62897-2

A CIP catalogue record for this book is available
from the British Library.

Printed and bound in China

10 9 8 7 6 5 4 3 2 1

Both metric and imperial measurements have been given
in all recipes. Use one set of measurements only, and not a
mixture of both.

Standard level spoon measurements are used in all recipes.
1 tablespoon = one 15 ml spoon
1 teaspoon = one 5 ml spoon

Ovens should be preheated to the specified temperature
– if using a fan-assisted oven, follow the manufacturer's
instructions for adjusting the time and temperature.

Fresh herbs should be used unless otherwise stated.

Medium eggs should be used unless otherwise stated.

The Department of Health advises that eggs should not
be consumed raw. This book contains some dishes made
with raw or lightly cooked eggs. It is prudent for vulnerable
people such as pregnant and nusing mothers, invalids,
the elderly, babies and young children to avoid uncooked
or lightly cooked dishes made with eggs. Once prepared,
these dishes should be kept refrigerated and used promptly.

This book includes dishes made with nuts and nut
derivatives. It is advisable for those with known allergic
reactions to nuts and nut derivatives and those who may
be potentially vulnerable to these allergies to avoid dishes
made with nuts and nut oils. It is also prudent to check the
labels of pre-prepared ingredients for the possible
inclusion of nut derivatives.

contents

introduction

introduction

this series

The Hamlyn All Colour Light Series is a collection of handy-sized books, each packed with over 200 healthy recipes on a variety of topics and cuisines to suit your needs.

The books are designed to help those people who are trying to lose weight by offering a range of delicious recipes that are low in calories but still high in flavour. The recipes show a calorie count per portion, so you will know exactly what you are eating. These are recipes for real and delicious food, not ultra-slimming meals, so they will help you maintain your new healthier eating plan for life. They must be used as part of a balanced diet, with the cakes and sweet dishes such as the ones in this book eaten only as an occasional treat.

how to use this book

All the recipes in this book are clearly marked with the number of calories (kcal) per serving. The chapters cover different calorie bands: under 500 calories, under 400 calories, etc.

There are variations on each recipe at the bottom of the page – note the calorie count as they do vary and can sometimes be more than the original recipe.

The figures assume that you are using low-fat versions of dairy products, so be sure to use skimmed milk and low-fat yogurt. Use moderate amounts of oil and butter for cooking and low-fat/low-calorie alternatives when you can.

Don't forget to take note of the number of portions each recipe makes and divide up the quantity of food accordingly, so that you know just how many calories you are consuming.

Be careful about sauces and accompaniments that will add to calorie content.

Above all, enjoy trying out the new flavours and exciting recipes that this book contains. Rather than dwelling on the thought that you are denying yourself your usual unhealthy treats, think of your new regime as a positive step towards a new you. Not only will you lose weight and feel more confident, but your health will benefit, the condition of your hair and nails will improve, and you will take on a healthy glow.

the risks of obesity

Up to half of women and two-thirds of men are overweight or obese in the developed world today. Being overweight can not only make us unhappy with our appearance, but can also lead to serious health problems.

When someone is obese, it means they are overweight to the point that it could start to seriously threaten their health. In fact, obesity ranks as a close second to smoking as a possible cause of cancer. Obese women are more likely to have complications during and after pregnancy, and people who are overweight or obese are also more likely to suffer from coronary heart disease, gallstones, osteoarthritis, high blood pressure and type 2 diabetes.

how can I tell if I am overweight?
The best way to tell if you are overweight is to work out your body mass index (BMI). If using metric measurements, divide your weight in kilograms (kg) by your height in metres (m) squared. (For example, if you are 1.7 m tall and weigh 70 kg, the calculation would be $70 \div 2.89 = 24.2$.) If using imperial measurements, divide your weight in pounds (lb) by your height in inches (in) squared and multiply by 703. Then compare the figure to the following list (these figures apply to healthy adults only).

Less than 20	underweight
20–25	healthy
25–30	overweight
Over 30	obese

As we all know by now, one of the major causes of obesity is eating too many calories.

what is a calorie?
Our bodies need energy to stay alive, grow, keep warm and be active. We get the energy we need to survive from the food and drinks we consume – more specifically, from the fat, carbohydrate, protein and alcohol that they contain.

A calorie (cal), as anyone who has ever been on a diet will know, is the unit used to measure

how much energy different foods contain. A calorie can be scientifically defined as the energy required to raise the temperature of 1 gram of water from 14.5°C to 15.5°C. A kilocaloric (kcal) is 1,000 calories and it is, in fact, kilocalories that we usually mean when we talk about the calories in different foods.

Different food types contain different numbers of calories. For example, a gram of carbohydrate (starch or sugar) provides 3.75 kcal, protein provides 4 kcal per gram, fat provides 9 kcal per gram and alcohol provides 7 kcal per gram.

So, fat is the most concentrated source of energy – weight for weight, it provides just over twice as many calories as protein or carbohydrate – with alcohol not far behind. The energy content of a food or drink depends on how many grams of carbohydrate, fat, protein and alcohol are present.

how many calories do we need?

The number of calories we need to consume varies from person to person, but your body weight is a clear indication of whether you are eating the right amount. Body weight is simply determined by the number of calories you are eating compared to the number of calories your body is using to maintain itself and needed for physical activity. If you regularly consume more calories than you use up, you will start to gain weight as extra energy is stored in the body as fat.

Based on our relatively inactive modern-day lifestyles, most nutritionists recommend that women should aim to consume around 2,000 calories (kcal) per day, and men around 2,500.

Of course, the amount of energy required depends on your level of activity: the more active you are, the more energy you need to maintain a stable weight.

a healthier lifestyle

To maintain a healthy body weight, we need to expend as much energy as we eat; to lose weight, energy expenditure must exceed calorie intake. So, exercise is a vital tool in the fight to lose weight. Physical activity doesn't just help us control body weight; it also helps to reduce our appetites and is known to have beneficial effects on the heart and blood that help prevent against cardiovascular disease.

Many of us claim we don't enjoy exercise and simply don't have the time to fit it into our hectic schedules. So the easiest way to increase physical activity is by incorporating it into our daily routines, perhaps by walking or cycling instead of driving (particularly for short journeys), taking up more active hobbies, and taking small and simple steps, such as using the stairs instead of the lift whenever possible.

As a general guide, adults should aim to undertake at least 30 minutes of moderate-intensity exercise, such as a brisk walk, five times a week. This does not have to be all at once: three sessions of 10 minutes are equally beneficial. Children and young people should be encouraged to take at least 60 minutes of moderate-intensity exercise every day.

Some activities will use up more energy than others. The following list shows some examples of the energy a person weighing 60 kg (132 lb) would expend doing the following activities for 30 minutes:

activity	energy
Ironing	69 kcal
Cleaning	75 kcal
Walking	99 kcal
Golf	129 kcal
Fast walking	150 kcal
Cycling	180 kcal
Aerobics	195 kcal
Swimming	195 kcal
Running	300 kcal
Sprinting	405 kcal

make changes for life

The best way to lose weight is to try to adopt healthier eating habits that you can easily maintain all the time, not just when you are trying to slim down. Aim to lose no more than 1 kg (2 lb) per week to ensure you lose only your fat stores. People who go on crash diets

lose lean muscle as well as fat and are much more likely to put the weight back on again soon afterwards.

For a woman, the aim is to reduce her daily calorie intake to around 1,500 kcal while she is trying to lose weight, then settle on around 2,000 per day thereafter to maintain her new body weight. Regular exercise will also make a huge difference: the more you can burn, the less you will need to diet.

improve your diet

For most of us, simply adopting a more balanced diet will reduce our calorie intake and lead to weight loss. Follow these simple recommendations:

Eat more starchy foods, such as bread, potatoes, rice and pasta. Assuming these replace the fattier foods you usually eat, and you don't smother them with oil or butter, this will help reduce the amount of fat and increase the amount of fibre in your diet. As a bonus, try to use wholegrain rice, pasta and flour, as the energy from these foods is released more slowly in the body, making you feel fuller for longer.

Eat more fruit and vegetables, aiming for at least five portions of different fruit and vegetables a day (excluding potatoes).

As long as you don't add extra fat to your fruit and vegetables in the form of cream, butter or oil, these changes will help reduce your fat intake and increase the amount of fibre and vitamins you consume.

Reduce the amount of fat in your diet, so you consume fewer calories. Choosing low-fat versions of dairy products, such as skimmed milk and low-fat yogurt, doesn't necessarily mean your food will be tasteless. Low-fat versions are available for most dairy products, including milk, cheese, crème fraîche, yogurt, and even cream and butter.

Choose lean cuts of meat, such as back bacon instead of streaky, and chicken breasts instead of thighs. Trim all visible fat off meat before cooking and avoid frying foods – grill or roast instead. Fish is also naturally low in fat and can make a variety of tempting dishes.

occasional healthy treats

While it is important when trying to lose weight to eat fewer sugary foods, such as biscuits, cakes and chocolate bars, there will be times when a sweet treat is called for: on special occasions and celebrations, for example. If you strive to eat healthily as a matter of course, the occasional dessert or piece of cake becomes a real treat and something to savour. Many of these recipes can be frozen in single portions then defrosted to be enjoyed later (see freezing instructions under 'storing cakes' on page 16).

simple steps to reduce your calorie intake

Few of us have an iron will, so when you are trying to cut down make it easier on yourself by following these steps:

- Serve small portions to start with. You may feel satisfied when you have finished, but if you are still hungry you can always go back for more.
- Once you have served up your meal, put away any leftover food before you eat. Don't put heaped serving dishes on the table as you will undoubtedly pick, even if you feel satisfied with what you have already eaten.
- Eat slowly and savour your food; then you are more likely to feel full when you have finished. If you rush a meal, you may still feel hungry afterwards.
- Make an effort with your meals. Just because you are cutting down doesn't mean your meals have to be low on taste as well as calories. You will feel more satisfied with a meal you have really enjoyed and will be less likely to look for comfort in a bag of crisps or a bar of chocolate.
- Plan your meals in advance to make sure you have all the ingredients you need. Casting around in the cupboards when you are hungry is unlikely to result in a healthy, balanced meal.
- Keep healthy and interesting snacks to hand for those moments when you need something to pep you up. You don't need to succumb to a chocolate bar if there are other tempting treats on offer.

Light cakes & desserts

Making your own cakes and desserts is rewarding and relaxing, and though such treats are generally considered off-limits when trying to eat healthily, the recipes in this book include many indulgent favourites that have been given a healthy make-over to keep them under 500, 400, 300 and even 200 calories per portion. These recipes are perfect to turn to when there is something to celebrate or you just feel in need of a treat – sometimes allowing yourself a small indulgence is an effective way to avoid abandoning a healthy eating regime in disgust. Homemade cakes and desserts surpass any shop-bought version, no matter how expensive, and are a highly personal way to spoil family and friends.

baking know-how

preparing your tins

Grease your cake tin by brushing on a little sunflower or vegetable oil, using a pastry brush, or by smearing a small knob of butter thinly over the inside of the tin. Even nonstick tins need a light greasing before use unless fully lined with nonstick baking paper.

Nonstick baking paper, as the name suggests, is nonstick and can be used to line tins or baking sheets without the addition of any oil or butter. Greaseproof paper must always be greased after shaping and pressing into a greased tin. It is usually easiest to brush it lightly with a little oil. Nonstick baking paper is preferable when lining baking sheets for meringues, roasting tins or deep round or square tins, where the base and side are lined.

cooking times

Cooking times are always a guide so do check on your cake's progress during cooking. Rely only on the oven's glass door if possible. Certainly, never open the door until just over halfway through cooking, when the cake will be set and at less risk of sinking. Even then, open it very slightly, just enough to see how

the cake is doing. If it is cooking more quickly at the front or sides, rotate the cake so it cooks evenly.

Cakes should be an even colour all over when cooked. Sponge cakes will spring back when gently pressed with fingertips. A fine skewer pushed into the middle of larger cakes should come out clean and dry.

tin sizes

Make sure you select the correct size tin for your cake. Tins should be measured across the base, especially if you are using a roasting dish as these normally have slightly sloping sides and a lip on the top edge.

storing cakes

Cakes or cookies are generally best kept in an airtight container and stored in a cool place, but store cakes with cream or cream cheese fillings or frostings in the fridge.

Most cakes freeze well although it's best to freeze those with glacé icing or fresh fruits unfilled or uniced. For very fragile cakes, freeze until firm then wrap in clingfilm or foil or pack into a plastic container. More robust cakes can be wrapped and then frozen. Large cakes can be sliced before freezing, and the slices interleaved with pieces of nonstick baking paper, so that just one or two slices can be thawed as required. Use all frozen cakes within 3 months, defrost at room

temperature for 2–4 hours depending on their size. Scones and cookies are best refreshed in the oven once defrosted, for 5–10 minutes at 180°C (350°F), Gas Mark 4.

troubleshooting

If your cake doesn't turn out as expected see if you can identify the problem from the following:

cake cracks heavily on top

- Cake cooked at too high a temperature or on too high an oven shelf.
- Rounded rather than level teaspoons of raising agent were used.
- Too small a tin was used so cake is very deep.

fruit sinks

- Too much fruit for the cake mixture to hold.
- Fruit was damp, or glacé cherries, if using, were very sticky with sugar.

cake sinks

- Oven door was opened before cake had set.
- Cake removed from oven before it was cooked right through.
- Too much raising agent so cake rose quickly but then collapsed before mixture was set.

cake does not rise properly

- Air was knocked out – perhaps the flour was stirred into a whisked cake rather than being gently folded in.
- Oven at too low a temperature or was

accidentally turned off.
- Raising agent such as baking powder was forgotten.
- Plain flour used in place of self-raising flour.
- Cake cooked in too large a tin.

cake is dry
- Not enough fat was incorporated.
- Cake was overcooked.
- Not wrapped and stored in a cake tin or plastic container after baking.

don't forget to...
- Use a pastry brush for greasing cake tins and glazing tops of scones.
- Preheat the oven, reducing the temperature by 10–20°C (50–68°F) if using a fan-assisted oven.
- Centre the oven shelf, unless you plan to cook on more than one baking sheet at a time.
- Grease and line the cake tins before you start.
- Use metric or imperial measurements, not a mixture of the two.
- Use level measuring spoons.
- Use a timer so that you know when to check on the cake's progress.

desserts know-how

whisking eggs and sugar
When making mousses, chilled soufflés, a Swiss roll or a sponge flan case, the recipe will call for the eggs and sugar to be whisked until the whisk leaves a trail when lifted above the mixture. This is best done with a hand-held electric mixer held over a bowl of eggs and sugar set over a saucepan of gently simmering water. The hot water helps to speed up the whisking process and increase the volume of trapped air in the eggs and sugar.

Three eggs will take 8–10 minutes to whisk until thick. To test when the mixture is ready, lift the whisk out of the mixture and try to drizzle a zigzag as the mixture falls from the whisk – if this stays on the surface for a few seconds, the mixture is ready.

whisking cream
Many people tend to overwhip double or whipping cream. The secret is to whisk the double cream until it just begins to form soft swirls, as it will thicken slightly as it stands. Overwhipping makes the cream take on a grainy, almost buttery texture and spoils the finish of the pudding.

folding in
Once a whisked mixture is ready, you will need to fold in pureed fruit, whipped cream or melted chocolate for a chilled soufflé or mousse, or sifted flour for a whisked sponge. Use a large-bowled spoon (a serving spoon is ideal) and gently cut and turn the spoon through the mixture in a figure-of-eight movement. Try to be as gentle as you can so that you don't knock out all the air you have just worked so hard to incorporate.

recipes
under 200
calories

french macaroons

Calories per serving **46**
Makes **24**
Preparation time **20 minutes**,
plus standing
Cooking time **10 minutes**

butter, for greasing
50 g (2 oz) **icing sugar**
65 g (2½ oz) **ground almonds**
2 **egg whites**
100 g (3½ oz) **caster sugar**
pink and **green food colouring**

Grease 2 baking sheets and line with nonstick baking paper.

Put the icing sugar in a food processor with the ground almonds and blend to a very fine consistency.

Put the egg whites in a thoroughly clean bowl and whisk until stiffly peaking. Gradually whisk in the caster sugar, a tablespoonful at a time and whisking well after each addition, until thick and very glossy. Divide the mixture equally between 2 bowls and add a few drops of food colouring to each bowl. Divide the almond mixture equally between the 2 bowls and use a metal spoon to stir the mixtures gently to combine.

Place 1 colour in a piping bag fitted with a 1 cm (½ inch) plain nozzle and pipe 12 x 3 cm (1¼ inch) rounds onto 1 baking sheet. Tap the baking sheet firmly to smooth the surfaces of the macaroons. Wash and dry the bag and piping nozzle and pipe 12 rounds in the second colour onto the other baking sheet. Leave to stand for 30 minutes.

Bake in a preheated oven, 160°C (325°F), Gas Mark 3, for about 15 minutes, or until the surfaces feel crisp. Leave to cool before carefully peeling away the paper.

pistachio biscotti

Calories per serving **53**
Makes about **24**
Preparation time **15 minutes**,
  plus cooling
Cooking time **30 minutes**

25 g (1 oz) **slightly salted
  butter**, softened
50 g (2 oz) **caster sugar**
finely grated rind of **1 lemon**
125 g (4 oz) **self-raising flour**
½ teaspoon **baking powder**
1 **egg yolk**
1 tablespoon **egg white**
65 g (2½ oz) **shelled
  pistachio nut**s, skinned and
  roughly chopped

Beat together the butter, sugar and lemon rind in a bowl
until pale and fluffy. Sift in the flour and baking powder,
then add the egg yolk, egg white and pistachios and mix
to a soft dough.

Divide the dough into 2 pieces and shape each into a
sausage about 15 cm (6 inches) long. Place the pieces,
well spaced apart, on a greased baking sheet and
flatten each to a depth of 1 cm (½ inch).

Bake in a preheated oven, 160°C (325°F), Gas Mark 3,
for 20 minutes until risen and turning pale golden.
Remove from the oven and leave to cool for 10 minutes,
leaving the oven on. Using a serrated knife, cut the
biscuits across into 1 cm (½ inch) thick slices. Return
to the baking sheet, cut sides face up, and bake for a
further 10 minutes to crisp up. Transfer to a wire rack
to cool.

For walnut oat cookies, mix together 50 g (2 oz)
sifted self-raising flour, 50 g (2 oz) porridge oats, 40 g
(1½ oz) chopped walnuts and ¼ teaspoon bicarbonate
of soda in a bowl. Put 50 g (2 oz) slightly salted butter,
50 g (2 oz) golden caster sugar and 1 tablespoon
golden syrup in a small saucepan. Heat gently until the
butter has melted. Add to the oat mixture and stir well to
mix. Roll teaspoonfuls of the mixture into small balls and
space well apart on a greased baking sheet. Bake as
above for about 15 minutes until pale golden. Transfer
to a wire rack to cool. **Calories per serving 53**

triple chocolate pretzels

Calories per serving **54**
Makes **40**
Preparation time **30 minutes**,
  plus rising and setting
Cooking time **6–8 minutes**

225 g (7½ oz) **strong white
  bread flour**
1 teaspoon **fast-action dried
  yeast**
2 teaspoons **caster sugar**
large pinch of **salt**
15 g (½ oz) melted **butter** or
  sunflower oil
125 ml (4 fl oz) warm **water**
75 g (3 oz) each plain d**ark,
  white** and **milk chocolate**,
  broken into pieces

Glaze
2 tablespoons **water**
½ teaspoon **salt**

Mix the flour, yeast, sugar and salt in a mixing bowl. Add the melted butter or oil and gradually mix in the warm water until you have a smooth dough. Knead the dough for 5 minutes on a lightly floured surface until smooth and elastic.

Cut the dough into quarters, then cut each quarter into 10 smaller pieces. Shape each piece into a thin rope about 20 cm (8 inches) long. Bend the rope so that it forms a wide arc, then bring one of the ends round in a loop and secure about halfway along the rope. Do the same with the other end, looping it across the first secured end.

Transfer the pretzels to 2 large greased baking sheets. Cover loosely with lightly oiled clingfilm and leave in a warm place for 30 minutes until well risen.

Make the glaze. Mix the water and salt in a bowl until the salt has dissolved, then brush this over the pretzels. Bake in a preheated oven, 200°C (400°F), Gas Mark 6, for 6–8 minutes until golden brown. Transfer to a wire rack to cool.

Melt the different chocolates in 3 separate heatproof bowls set over saucepans of gently simmering water. Drizzle random lines of dark chocolate over the pretzels, using a spoon. Leave to harden, then repeat with the white and then the milk chocolate.

For classic pretzels, brush plain pretzels as soon as they come out of the oven with a glaze made by heating 2 teaspoons salt, ½ teaspoon caster sugar and 2 tablespoons water in a saucepan until dissolved. **Calories per serving 22**

blueberry friands

Calories per serving **65**
Makes **16**
Preparation time **10 minutes**
Cooking time **15 minutes**

50 g (2 oz) **lightly salted butter**
2 **egg whites**
25 g (1 oz) **plain flour**
75 g (3 oz) **icing sugar**, plus extra for dusting
40 g (1 ½ oz) **ground almonds**
½ teaspoon **almond extract**
50 g (2 oz) **blueberries**

Place 16 mini silicone muffin cases on a baking sheet.

Melt the butter and leave to cool. Whisk the egg whites in a thoroughly clean bowl until frothy but not turning white and peaking.

Sift the flour and icing sugar into the bowl, then add the ground almonds. Stir the almond extract into the melted butter and add to the bowl. Using a large metal spoon, stir the ingredients gently together until combined. Divide among the cases so each is about three-quarters full and place several blueberries on top of each.

Bake in a preheated oven, 200°C (400°F), Gas Mark 6, for 12–15 minutes until risen and just firm to the touch. Leave in the cases for 5 minutes, then transfer to a wire rack to cool. Serve warm or cold, dusted with icing sugar.

For hazelnut & apricot friands, lightly toast 40 g (1 ½ oz) hazelnuts and grind in a food processor. Chop 50 g (2 oz) plump dried apricots into very small pieces. Prepare the cakes as above using the hazelnuts instead of the almonds, vanilla extract instead of the almond extract and placing a little pile of chopped apricots in the centres instead of the blueberries. **Calories per serving 70**

seeded oatcakes

Calories per serving **65**
Makes **20**
Preparation time **15 minutes**
Cooking time **25 minutes**

125 g (4 oz) **medium oatmeal**
75 g (3 oz) **plain flour**
4 tablespoons **mixed seeds**,
   such as **poppy seeds**,
   linseeds and **sesame
   seeds**
½ teaspoon **celery salt** or
   sea salt
½ teaspoon **freshly ground
   black pepper**
50 g (2 oz) **unsalted butter**,
   chilled and diced
5 tablespoons **cold water**

Put the oatmeal, flour, seeds, salt and pepper in a
bowl or food processor. Add the butter and rub in with
the fingertips or process until the mixture resembles
breadcrumbs. Add the measured water and mix or blend
to a firm dough, adding a little more water if the dough
feels dry.

Roll out the dough on a lightly floured surface to
2.5 mm (⅛ inch) thick. Cut out 20 rounds using a 6 cm
(2½ inch) plain or fluted biscuit cutter, re-rolling the
trimmings to make more. Place slightly apart on a large
greased baking sheet.

Bake in a preheated oven, 180°C (350°F), Gas Mark 4,
for about 25 minutes until firm. Transfer to a wire rack
to cool. Serve with cheese.

For crushed spice biscuits, crush ½ teaspoon cumin
seeds, ½ teaspoon coriander seeds and ¼ teaspoon
dried chilli flakes using a pestle and mortar or a small
bowl and the end of a rolling pin. Finely chop 25 g
(1 oz) ready-to-eat dried apricots. Make the biscuits as
above, omitting the seeds and celery salt and adding the
crushed spices and apricots. Serve with soft cheeses.
Calories per serving 59

lemon & cardamom madeleines

Calories per serving **80**
Makes **about 30**
Preparation time **20 minutes,**
  plus setting
Cooking time **30 minutes**

125 g (4 oz) **lightly salted**
  butter, melted, plus extra for
  greasing
125 g (4 oz) **self-raising**
  flour, plus extra for dusting
2 teaspoons **cardamom pods**
3 **eggs**
125 g (4 oz) **caster sugar**
finely grated **zest** of 1 **lemon**
½ teaspoon **baking powder**

Glaze
2 tablespoons **lemon juice**
75 g (3 oz) **icing sugar**, sifted,
  plus extra for dusting

Grease a madeleine tray with melted butter and dust with flour. Tap out the excess flour.

Crush the cardamom pods using a pestle and mortar to release the seeds. Remove the shells and crush the seeds a little further.

Put the eggs, caster sugar, lemon zest and crushed cardamom seeds in a heatproof bowl and rest the bowl over a saucepan of gently simmering water. Whisk with a hand-held electric whisk until the mixture is thick and pale and the mixture leaves a trail when lifted.

Sift the flour and baking powder into the bowl and gently fold in using a large metal spoon. Drizzle the melted butter around the edges of the mixture and fold the ingredients together to combine. Spoon the mixture into the madeleine sections until about two-thirds full. (Keep the remaining mixture for a second batch.)

Bake in a preheated oven, 220°C (425°F), Gas Mark 7, for about 10 minutes until risen and golden. Leave in the tray for 5 minutes, then transfer to a wire rack.

Make the glaze by putting the lemon juice in a bowl and beating in the icing sugar. Brush over the madeleines and leave to set. Serve lightly dusted with icing sugar.

For espresso madeleines with coffee glaze, mix 1 teaspoon instant espresso coffee powder with 2 teaspoons hot water. Make the madeleines, adding the coffee mixture once the whisk leaves a trail. Bake as above. Mix ½ teaspoon espresso coffee powder with 2 teaspoons hot water. Beat with 50 g (2 oz) sifted icing sugar until smooth and brush over the madeleines.
Calories per serving 76

raspberry ripple meringues

Calories per serving **81**
Makes about **12**
Preparation time **15 minutes**
Cooking time 1¼ **hours**

40 g (1½ oz) **fresh
    raspberries**, plus extra to
    serve (optional)
2 tablespoons **raspberry jam**
4 **egg whites**
200 g (7 oz) **caster sugar**

Put the raspberries in a bowl and mash with a fork until broken up and turning juicy. Add the jam and mash together to make a purée. Tip into a sieve resting over a small bowl and press the purée with the back of a spoon to extract as much juice as possible.

Whisk the egg whites in a large clean bowl with a hand-held electric whisk until peaking. Whisk in a tablespoonful of the sugar and continue to whisk for about 15 seconds. Gradually add the remaining sugar, a spoonful at a time, until thick and glossy.

Drizzle over the raspberry purée and lightly stir in using a spatula or large metal spoon, scooping up the meringue from the base of the bowl so that the mixture is streaked with the purée. Take care not to over-mix.

Drop large spoonfuls of the mixture, each about the size of a small orange, on to a large baking sheet lined with baking parchment, then swirl with the back of a teaspoon. Bake in a preheated oven, 120°C (250°F), Gas Mark ½, for about 1¼ hours or until the meringues are crisp and come away easily from the paper. Leave to cool on the paper. Serve with extra raspberries, if liked.

For gingerbread meringues, put 5 tablespoons black treacle in a small bowl, stir in 2 teaspoons ground ginger, 1 teaspoon ground mixed spice and 1 teaspoon boiling water and mix well. Make the meringue mixture as above, replacing 50 g (2 oz) of the caster sugar with 50 g (2 oz) dark muscovado sugar, then ripple with the treacle syrup instead of the raspberry purée. Bake as above. **Calories per serving 93**

fresh melon sorbet

Calories per serving **86**

Serves **4**

Preparation time **15 minutes**, plus freezing

1 **cantaloupe melon**, weighing 1 kg (2 lb)

50 g (2 oz) **icing sugar**

juice of **1 lime** or **small lemon**

1 **egg white**

Cut the melon in half and scoop out and discard the seeds. Scoop out the melon flesh with a spoon and discard the shells.

Place the flesh in a food processor or blender with the icing sugar and lime or lemon juice and process to a purée. (Alternatively, rub through a sieve.) Pour into a freezer container, cover and freeze for 2–3 hours.

If using an ice-cream machine, purée, then pour into the machine, churn and freeze until half-frozen.

Whisk the melon mixture to break up the ice crystals. Then whisk the egg white until stiff and whisk it into the half-frozen melon mixture. Return to the freezer until firm. Alternatively, add whisked egg white to the ice-cream machine and churn until very thick.

Transfer the sorbet to the fridge 20 minutes before serving to soften slightly or scoop straight from the ice-cream machine. Scoop the sorbet into glass dishes to serve. To make differently coloured sorbet, make up three batches of sorbet using a cantaloupe melon in one and honeydew and watermelon in the others.

For gingered melon sorbet, peel and finely grate a 2.5 cm (1 inch) piece of root ginger, then stir into the melon purée. Scoop into small glasses and drizzle each glass with 1 tablespoon ginger wine. **Calories per serving 92**

fruited griddle cakes

Calories per serving **86**
Makes **30**
Preparation time **25 minutes**
Cooking time **18 minutes**

250 g (8 oz) **self-raising flour**
125 g (4 oz) **butter**, diced
100 g (3½ oz) **caster sugar**,
  plus extra for sprinkling
50 g (2 oz) **currants**
50 g (2 oz) **sultanas**
1 teaspoon **ground mixed
  spice**
grated rind of ½ **lemon**
1 **egg**, beaten
1 tablespoon **milk**, if needed
oil, for greasing

Put the flour in a mixing bowl or a food processor. Add the butter and rub in with your fingertips or process until the mixture resembles fine breadcrumbs. Stir in the sugar, dried fruit, spice and lemon rind.

Add the egg, then gradually mix in milk, if needed, to make a smooth dough. Knead lightly, then roll out on a lightly floured surface until 5 mm (¼ inch) thick. Stamp out 5 cm (2 inch) circles using a fluted round biscuit cutter. Reknead the trimmings and continue rolling and stamping out until all the dough has been used.

Pour a little oil on to a piece of folded kitchen paper and use to grease a griddle or heavy nonstick frying pan. Heat the pan, then add the cakes in batches, regreasing the griddle or pan as needed, and fry over a medium to low heat for about 3 minutes each side until golden brown and cooked through. Serve warm, sprinkled with a little extra sugar or spread with butter, if liked. Store in an airtight tin for up to 2 days.

For orange & cinnamon griddle cakes, use the grated rind of ½ orange instead of the lemon, and 1 teaspoon ground cinnamon in place of the mixed spice. Continue the recipe as above. **Calories per serving 86**

honey, grape & cinnamon tartlets

Calories per serving **96**
Makes **16**
Preparation time **25 minutes,
plus cooling**
Cooking time **10 minutes**

100 g (3½ oz) **seedless red
grapes,** peeled and halved
100 g (3½ oz) **seedless
white grapes,** peeled and
halved
3 tablespoons **dessert wine**
or **grape juice**
25 g (1 oz) **unsalted butter,**
melted
½ teaspoon **ground
cinnamon**
3 sheets of **filo pastry**
flour, for dusting
100 ml (3½ fl oz) **double
cream**
100 ml (3½ fl oz) **Greek
yogurt**
2 tablespoons **clear honey,**
plus extra to drizzle

Place 16 mini silicone muffin cases on a baking sheet.

Put the grapes in a bowl with the wine or grape juice.
Mix the melted butter with the cinnamon.

Unfold the pastry sheets on a lightly floured surface,
then put one in front of you (covering the others with
clingfilm). Cut into 6.5 cm (2¾ inch) squares. Brush
the squares lightly with the spiced butter. Cut out more
squares from the other 2 sheets and position over the
first, adjusting the positions so the points are evenly
staggered. Press into the cases and brush with a little
more butter.

Bake in a preheated oven, 190°C (375°F), Gas Mark 5,
for 10 minutes until golden. Transfer to a wire rack.

Beat the cream with the yogurt and honey until just
holding its shape. Drain the grapes over the cream so
you can beat the juice into the cream. Spoon the cream
mixture into the pastry cases and pile the grapes on top.
Serve drizzled with extra honey.

For blueberry & cream cheese tartlets, make the
filo cases as above, omitting the cinnamon from the
butter. Beat 250 g (8 oz) cream cheese in a bowl with
1 teaspoon vanilla bean paste and 2 tablespoons sifted
icing sugar until smooth. Spoon into the cases and top
with blueberry conserve. Serve lightly dusted with icing
sugar. **Calories per serving 102**

easy almond macaroons

Calories per serving **98**
Makes about **15**
Preparation time **10 minutes**
Cooking time **15 minutes**

2 **egg whites**
100 g (3½ oz) **golden caster
sugar**
100 g (3½ oz) **ground
almonds**
blanched almonds, to
decorate

Whisk the egg whites in a clean bowl with a hand-held electric whisk until peaking. Gradually whisk in the sugar, a spoonful at a time, until thick and glossy. Add the ground almonds and stir in until combined.

Drop dessertspoonfuls of the mixture, slightly apart, on a large baking sheet lined with baking parchment. Press an almond on top of each.

Bake in a preheated oven, 180°C (350°F), Gas Mark 4, for about 15 minutes until the biscuits are pale golden and just crisp. Leave on the paper for 5 minutes, then transfer to a wire rack to cool.

For scribbled chocolate macaroons, make the macaroons as above, replacing 20 g (¾ oz) of the ground almonds with 20 g (¾ oz) cocoa powder and omitting the whole almonds. Melt 50 g (2 oz) plain dark or milk chocolate, then drizzle over the cooled biscuits with a teaspoon. **Calories per serving 103**

balsamic strawberries & mango

Calories per serving **100**
Serves **4**
Preparation time **5 minutes**,
  plus overnight chilling and
  standing

500 g (1 lb) **strawberries**,
  thickly sliced
1 large **mango**, peeled, stoned
  and sliced
1−2 tablespoons **caster
  sugar**, to taste
3 tablespoons **balsamic
  vinegar**
2 tablespoons chopped **fresh
  mint**, to decorate

Mix together the strawberries and mango in a large, shallow bowl, sprinkle with the sugar, according to taste, and pour over the balsamic vinegar. Cover with clingfilm and chill overnight.

Remove the fruit from the refrigerator and leave to stand for at least 1 hour before serving.

Spoon the fruit into serving bowls, drizzle over the syrup and serve, sprinkled with the mint.

For peppery strawberries & blueberries, mix the strawberries with 125 g (4 oz) blueberries and make as above. Sprinkle with a few grinds of black pepper and the chopped mint before serving. **Calories per serving 76**

marshmallow crackle squares

Calories per serving **102**
Cuts into **14**
Preparation time **10 minutes**,
  plus setting
Cooking time **5 minutes**

200 g (7 oz) **marshmallows**,
  halved
40 g (1 ½ oz) **unsalted butter**,
  diced
100 g (3½ oz) **crisped rice
  cereal**
pink sugar sprinkles, to
  decorate

Reserve 50 g (2 oz) of the white marshmallows. Put 25 g (1 oz) of the butter and the remaining marshmallows into a saucepan and heat very gently until melted. Remove from the heat and stir in the cereal until evenly coated.

Spoon the mixture into an 18 cm (7 inch) square shallow baking tin, greased and lined with baking parchment, and pack down firmly with the back of a lightly oiled spoon.

Place the remaining butter and reserved marshmallows in a small saucepan and heat gently until melted. Drizzle into the tin in lines, then scatter the sprinkles over the top. Leave in a cool place for 2 hours or until firm. Turn out of the tin on to a board, peel off the lining paper and cut into small squares.

For chocolate crackle cakes, melt 100 g (3½ oz) milk chocolate, broken into pieces, and 1 tablespoon golden syrup in a heatproof bowl set over a saucepan of gently simmering water (don't let the base of the bowl touch the water). Put 100 g (3½ oz) cornflakes in a plastic bag and crush lightly using a rolling pin. Tip into the chocolate mixture and stir well until thoroughly combined. Pack into 14–16 small paper cupcake cases and top with chocolate sprinkles. Leave to set for at least 1 hour before serving. **Calories per serving 79**

figs with yogurt & honey

Calories per serving **105**
Serves **4**
Preparation time **5 minutes**
Cooking time **10 minutes**

8 ripe **figs**
4 tablespoons **natural yogurt**
2 tablespoons **clear honey**

Slice the figs in half and place on a hot griddle pan, skin-side down. Sear for 10 minutes until the skins begin to blacken, then remove.

Arrange the figs on 4 plates and serve with a spoonful of yogurt and some honey spooned over the top.

For brioche French toasts with figs, yogurt & honey, brush 4 slices brioche with a mixture of 50 g (2 oz) melted butter and 50 ml (2 fl oz) single cream and toast under a grill. Top with figs, as above. **Calories per serving 347**

poached peaches & raspberries

Calories per serving **107**
Serves **6**
Preparation time **15 minutes**
Cooking time **25 minutes**

250 ml (8 fl oz) **water**
150 ml (¼ pint) **marsala** or
  sweet sherry
75 g (3 oz) **caster sugar**
1 **vanilla pod**
6 **peaches**, halved and pitted
150 g (5 oz) **fresh**
  raspberries

Pour the measured water and marsala or sherry into a saucepan, then add the sugar. Slit the vanilla pod lengthways and scrape out the black seeds from inside the pod. Add these to the water with the pod, then gently heat the mixture until the sugar has dissolved.

Place the peach halves in an ovenproof dish so that they sit together snugly. Pour over the hot syrup, then cover and cook in a preheated oven, 180°F (350°F), Gas Mark 4, for 20 minutes.

Scatter over the raspberries. Serve the fruit either warm or cold. Spoon into serving bowls and decorate with the vanilla pod cut into thin strips.

For poached prunes with vanilla, make the sugar syrup as above, then add 250 g (8 oz) dried pitted prunes instead of the peaches. Cover and simmer as above, then serve warm with spoonfuls of crème fraîche and 4 crumbled amaretti biscuits, if liked. **Calories per serving 156** (not including crème fraîche and amaretti)

scrabble cookies

Calories per serving **108**
Makes **30**
Preparation time **35 minutes**
Cooking time **5 minutes**, plus
   chilling and cooling

75 g (3 oz) **unsalted butter**,
   softened, plus extra for
   greasing
75 g (3 oz) **caster sugar**
1 **egg**
½ teaspoon **vanilla extract**
250 g (8 oz) **plain flour**, sifted,
   plus extra for dusting

To decorate
375 g (12 oz) **ready-to-roll
   icing**
icing sugar, for dusting
2–3 tablespoons **apricot jam**,
   sieved
1 small tube of **coloured
   writing icing**

Grease 2 baking sheets and line with nonstick baking paper. Beat together the butter and sugar until pale and fluffy. Gradually beat in the egg and vanilla extract, adding a little flour to prevent the mixture curdling. Add the flour and fold in to make a stiff dough. Wrap in clingfilm and refrigerate for 20 minutes.

Roll out the dough on a lightly floured surface to 2.5 mm (⅛ inch) thick. Cut out about 30 rounds, using a 4–5 cm (1½–2 inch) diameter cookie cutter, rerolling the trimmings as necessary. Place on the baking sheets.

Bake in a preheated oven, 180°C (350°F), Gas Mark 4, for 5 minutes, or until a pale golden colour. Transfer to a wire rack and leave to cool. Roll out the icing on a sugar-dusted surface until 2.5 mm (⅛ inch) thick. Using the same cutter as before, dusted this time with a little icing sugar, cut out the same number of circles. Using a clean paintbrush, paint a little of the sieved jam on each cookie to ensure that the icing will stick, then place the icing shapes on the cookies and press down lightly. Using the coloured writing icing, write a letter on each cookie to spell out the name or message.

For homemade ready-to-roll icing, put 1 tablespoon egg white in a bowl with 1 tablespoon liquid glucose and 100 g (3½ oz) sifted icing sugar and beat to a smooth paste. Gradually work in a further 150 g (5 oz) icing sugar, stirring well until the mixture is very firm. Turn out onto the work surface and knead to a smooth paste, which should be firm and rollable, not sticky. Work in a little more icing sugar if necessary. Wrap tightly in several thicknesses of clingfilm and store until ready. **Calories per serving 33**

banana & sultana drop scones

Calories per serving **110**
Makes **10**
Preparation time **10 minutes**
Cooking time **8 minutes**

125 g (4 oz) **self-raising flour**
2 tablespoons **caster sugar**
½ teaspoon **baking powder**
1 small ripe **banana**, about
   125 g (4 oz) with skin on,
   peeled and roughly mashed
1 **egg**, beaten
150 ml (¼ pint) **milk**
50 g (2 oz) **sultanas**
oil, for greasing
butter, clear honey, golden or
   maple syrup, to serve

Put the flour, sugar and baking powder in a mixing bowl. Add the mashed banana with the egg. Gradually whisk in the milk with a fork until the mixture resembles a smooth thick batter. Stir in the sultanas.

Pour a little oil on to a piece of folded kitchen paper and use to grease a griddle or heavy nonstick frying pan. Heat the pan, then drop heaped dessertspoonfuls of the mixture, well spaced apart, on to the pan. Cook for 2 minutes until bubbles appear on the top and the undersides are golden. Turn over and cook for 1–2 minutes more until the second side is done.

Serve warm, topped with 1 teaspoon butter, honey, golden or maple syrup per scone. These are best eaten on the day they are made.

For summer berry drop scones, make the above recipe in the same way but stir in 125 g (4 oz) mixed fresh blueberries and raspberries instead of the sultanas. **Calories per serving 101**

banana & muscovado ripples

Calories per serving **112**
Serves **4**
Preparation time **5 minutes**,
  plus standing

2 ripe **bananas**
juice of ½ **lemon**
15 g (½ oz) crystallized or
  glacé **ginger**, finely chopped,
  plus extra to decorate
150 g (5 oz) **low-fat natural
  yogurt**
8 teaspoons dark **muscovado
  sugar**

Toss the bananas in a little lemon juice and mash on
a plate with a fork. Add the ginger and yogurt and mix
together. Spoon one-third of the mixture into the bases
of 4 small dessert glasses.

Sprinkle 1 teaspoon of the sugar over each dessert.
Spoon half of the remaining banana mixture on top,
then repeat with a second layer of sugar. Complete the
layers with the remaining banana mixture and decorate
with a little extra ginger, cut into slightly larger pieces.

Leave the puddings to stand for 10–15 minutes for
the sugar to dissolve and form a syrupy layer between
the layers of banana yogurt. Serve with dainty biscuits,
if liked.

For banana, apricot & cardamom ripples, cook
100 g (3½ oz) ready-to-eat dried apricots with 150 ml
(¼ pint) water and 2 roughly crushed cardamom pods,
adding the pods and their black seeds, in a covered
saucepan for 10 minutes until tender. Remove and
discard the cardamom pods, then purée the mixture
with 3 tablespoons fresh orange juice. Cool, then layer
with banana and the yogurt mix as above. This can be
served immediately. **Calories per serving 122**

pomegranate & ginger slice

Calories per serving **121**
Cuts into **20**
Preparation time **25 minutes**
Cooking time **50 minutes**

200 g (7 oz) **plain flour**
1 teaspoon **bicarbonate of soda**
100 ml (3½ fl oz) **milk**
1 **egg**
100 g (3½ oz) **dark muscovado sugar**
125 g (4 oz) **black treacle**
75 g (3 oz) **unsalted butter**
3 pieces of **stem ginger in syrup**, chopped

For the topping
300 ml (½ pint) **pomegranate juice**
2 tablespoons **clear honey**
1 **pomegranate**

Sift the flour and bicarbonate of soda into a bowl. Beat together the milk and egg in a jug. Put the sugar, treacle and butter in a saucepan and heat gently until the butter melts and the sugar dissolves. Remove from the heat and add to the milk mixture with the chopped ginger. Add to the dry ingredients and stir together using a large metal spoon until well combined.

Spoon the mixture into 2 greased and lined 1 kg (2 lb) or 1.3 litre (2¼ pint) loaf tins and level the surface. Bake in a preheated oven, 160°C (325°F), Gas Mark 3, for 30 minutes or until just firm to the touch and a skewer inserted into the centre comes out clean. Leave to cool in the tins, then loosen at the ends and transfer to a wire rack. Peel off the lining paper.

Make the topping. Pour the pomegranate juice into a saucepan and bring to the boil, then boil for about 15 minutes until thick and syrupy and reduced to about 3 tablespoons. Stir in the honey. Halve the pomegranate and push the halves inside out to release the fleshy seeds, discarding any white membrane. Scatter the seeds over the top of the cakes. Drizzle with the syrup and cut into small squares to serve.

For sultana & lemon gingerbread, make the cakes as above, reducing the milk by 25 ml (1 fl oz) and sprinkling 75 g (3 oz) sultanas over the mixture in the tins. For the icing, mix together 75 g (3 oz) sifted golden icing sugar and 2 teaspoons lemon juice in a bowl to make a smooth, spoonable icing, then drizzle in lines over the cooled cakes. **Calories per serving 146**

chocolate florentines

Calories per serving **126**
Makes **26**
Preparation time **30 minutes**
Cooking time **15–20 minutes**

100 g (3½ oz) **butter**
100 g (3½ oz) **caster sugar**
75 g (3 oz) multi-coloured
  glacé cherries, roughly
  chopped
75 g (3 oz) **flaked almonds**
50 g (2 oz) whole **candied
  peel**, finely chopped
50 g (2 oz) **hazelnuts**, roughly
  chopped
2 tablespoons **plain flour**
150 g (5 oz) plain **dark
  chocolate**, broken into
  pieces

Put the butter and sugar in a saucepan and heat gently until the butter has melted and the sugar dissolved. Remove the pan from the heat and stir in all the remaining ingredients except the chocolate.

Spoon tablespoons of the mixture, well spaced apart, on to 3 baking sheets lined with nonstick baking paper. Flatten the mounds slightly. Cook one baking sheet at a time in the centre of a preheated oven, 180°C (350°F), Gas Mark 4, for 5–7 minutes until the nuts are golden.

After removing each baking sheet from the oven, neaten and shape the cooked biscuits by placing a slightly larger plain round biscuit cutter over the top and rotating to smooth and tidy up the edges. Leave to cool.

Melt the chocolate in a heatproof bowl set over a saucepan of gently simmering water. Peel the biscuits off the lining paper and arrange upside down on a wire rack. Spoon the melted chocolate over the flat underside of the biscuits and spread the surfaces level. Leave to cool and harden.

For white chocolate & ginger florentines, add 2 tablespoons ready-chopped glacé ginger to the glacé and candied fruit and nut mixture. Spread the cooked biscuits with melted white chocolate instead of plain dark chocolate as above. **Calories per serving 125**

passion fruit panna cotta

Calories per serving **127**
Serves **4**
Preparation time **20 minutes**,
  plus setting

2 **gelatine leaves**
8 **passion fruit**
200 g (7 oz) **half-fat crème
  fraîche**
125 g (4 oz) **fat-free Greek
  yogurt**
1 teaspoon **caster sugar**
vanilla pod, split

Soften the gelatine leaves in cold water. Halve the passion fruit and remove the seeds, working over a bowl to catch as much juice as you can. Reserve the seeds for decoration.

Combine the crème fraîche, yogurt and passion fruit juice.

Put 100 ml (3½ fl oz) water in a small saucepan, add the sugar and the seeds from the vanilla pod and heat gently, stirring until the sugar has dissolved. Drain the gelatine and add to the pan. Stir until dissolved, then leave to cool to room temperature.

Mix the gelatine mixture into the crème fraîche, then pour into 4 ramekins or moulds. Refrigerate for 6 hours or until set.

Turn the panna cotta out of their moulds by briefly immersing each ramekin in very hot water. Spoon over the reserved seeds to decorate.

For coffee panna cotta, substitute 2 teaspoons strong coffee for the passion fruit and continue as for the recipe, using the vanilla pod. Decorate each panna cotta with chocolate coffee beans, if liked. **Calories per serving 105**

mint granita

Calories per serving **136**
Serves **6**
Preparation time **20 minutes**,
  plus cooling and freezing
Cooking time **4 minutes**

200 g (7 oz) **caster sugar**
300 ml (½ pint) **water**, plus
  extra to top up
pared zest and juice of 3
  lemons
25 g (1 oz) **fresh mint**, plus
  a few sprigs to decorate
icing sugar, for dusting

Put the sugar and measured water into a saucepan, add the lemon zest and gently heat until the sugar has dissolved. Increase the heat and boil for 2 minutes.

Tear the tips off the mint stems and finely chop to give about 3 tablespoons, then reserve. Add the larger mint leaves and stems to the hot syrup and leave for 1 hour to cool and for the flavours to develop.

Strain the syrup into a jug, add the chopped mint and lemon juice and top up to 600 ml (1 pint) with extra cold water. Pour into a small roasting tin and freeze the mixture for 2–3 hours or until mushy.

Break up the ice crystals with a fork, then return to the freezer for 2–3 more hours, breaking up with a fork once or twice until the mixture is the consistency of crushed ice. Serve now, spooned into small glass tumblers, decorated with tiny sprigs of mint dusted with icing sugar, or leave in the freezer until required. If leaving in the freezer, allow to soften for 15 minutes before serving. If frozen overnight or longer, break up with a fork before serving.

For iced ruby grapefruit granita, make a plain sugar syrup as above, omitting the lemon zest. When cool, halve 4 ruby grapefruits, squeeze the juice and reserve 4 halved shells. Strain the juice into the syrup instead of the lemon juice, then freeze as above. Serve the dessert spooned into the reserved grapefruit shells. **Calories per serving 143**

cardamom & orange biscuits

Calories per serving **153**
Makes about **12**
Preparation time **15 minutes**,
  plus chilling
Cooking time **15 minutes**

12 **cardamom pods**
150 g (5 oz) **plain flour**
100 g (3½ oz) **slightly salted
  butter**, chilled and diced
50 g (2 oz) **icing sugar**, sifted
1 **egg yolk**
finely grated rind of **1 orange**

For the icing
75 g (3 oz) **icing sugar**, sifted
1 tablespoon **orange juice**

Crush the cardamom pods using a pestle and mortar or a small bowl and the end of a rolling pin. Discard the shells and crush the seeds as finely as possible.

Put the flour and crushed seeds in a bowl or food processor. Add the butter and rub in with the fingertips or process until the mixture resembles coarse breadcrumbs. Add the icing sugar and stir in or blend briefly. Add the egg yolk and orange rind and mix or blend to a dough. Wrap in clingfilm and chill for 1 hour.

Roll out the dough on a lightly floured surface to 5 mm (¼ inch) thick. Cut out about 12 heart shapes using a 5–6 cm (2–2½ inch) heart biscuit cutter, re-rolling the trimmings to make more. Place slightly apart on a large greased baking sheet and bake in a preheated oven, 190°C (375°F), Gas Mark 5, for about 15 minutes until pale golden. Transfer to a wire rack to cool.

Make the icing. Beat together the icing sugar and orange juice in a bowl to make a smooth, thin icing. Drizzle lines of icing over the biscuits to decorate.

For vanilla dessert biscuits, make and chill the dough as above, omitting the cardamom and replacing the orange rind with 1 teaspoon vanilla bean paste or extract. Roll out as above and cut out about 12 rounds using a 5–6 cm (2–2½ inch) plain biscuit cutter. Bake as above and serve lightly dusted with sifted icing sugar. **Calories per serving 134**

green fruit salad

Calories per serving **167**

Serves **6**

Preparation time **15 minutes**

300 g (10 oz) **seedless green grapes**, halved

4 **kiwifruits**, peeled, quartered and sliced

2 **ripe pears**, peeled, cored and sliced

4 **passion fruits**, halved

4 tablespoons concentrated **elderflower cordial**

4 tablespoons **water**

300 g (10 oz) **Greek yogurt**

2 tablespoons **runny honey**

Put the grapes, kiwifruits and pears in a bowl. Using a teaspoon, scoop the seeds from 3 of the passion fruits into the bowl. Mix 2 tablespoons of the cordial with the measured water and drizzle over the salad. Gently toss together and spoon into 6 glass tumblers.

Stir the remaining undiluted cordial into the yogurt, then mix in the honey. Spoon into the glasses.

Decorate with the remaining passion fruit seeds and serve.

For ruby fruit salad, mix 300 g (10 oz) halved seedless red grapes with 150 g (5 oz) fresh raspberries and 150 g (5 oz) sliced strawberries. Sprinkle with the seeds from ½ pomegranate, then drizzle with 6 tablespoons red grape juice. Mix the yogurt with honey only, then spoon over the fruit salad. Decorate with a few extra pomegranate seeds. **Calories per serving 123**

creamy mango & passion fruit

Calories per serving **168** (plus 46 calories for biscuits)

Serves **4**

Preparation time **10 minutes**

1 large **mango**, peeled, stoned and cut into chunks

750 g (1½ lb) **fat-free natural yogurt**

1–2 tablespoons **agave nectar**, to taste

1 **vanilla pod**, split in half lengthways

4 **passion fruit**, halved

Place the mango in a food processor or blender and blend to a purée.

Put the yogurt and agave nectar, according to taste, in a large bowl, scrape in the seeds from the vanilla pod and beat together. Gently fold in the mango purée and spoon into tall glasses or glass serving dishes.

Scoop the seeds from the passion fruit and spoon over the mango yogurt. Serve immediately, with 2 thin biscuits, if liked.

For blackcurrant & almond yogurt, purée 250 g (8 oz) blackcurrants as above and fold into the yogurt with the agave nectar, according to taste, and 1 teaspoon almond essence. Spoon into tall serving glasses and scatter with toasted almonds, to serve. **Calories per serving 173**

grilled fruits with palm sugar

Calories per serving **176**
Serves **4**
Preparation time **10 minutes**
Cooking time **6–16 minutes**

25 g (1 oz) **palm sugar**
grated rind and juice of
  1 **lime**
2 tablespoons **water**
½ teaspoon **cracked black**
  peppercorns
500 g (1 lb) mixed prepared
  fruits, such as **pineapple**
  or **peach** slices or **mango**
  wedges

To serve
cinnamon or **vanilla ice**
  cream
lime slices

Put the sugar, lime rind and juice, measured water and peppercorns in a small saucepan and heat over a low heat until the sugar has dissolved. Plunge the base of the pan into iced water to cool.

Brush the cooled syrup over the prepared fruits and cook under a preheated hot grill for 6–8 minutes on each side, or over a preheated hot gas barbecue or the hot coals of a charcoal barbecue, for 3–4 minutes on each side until charred and tender.

Serve with scoops of cinnamon or vanilla ice cream and lime slices.

For grilled fruit kebabs, cut the prepared fruits into large chunks, thread on to wooden skewers, presoaked in cold water for 30 minutes, and brush with the cooled syrup before cooking as in the recipe above. **Calories per serving 176**

raspberry shortbread mess

Calories per serving **177**
Serves **4**
Preparation time **5 minutes**

300 g (10 oz) **raspberries**,
  roughly chopped
4 **shortbread fingers**, roughly
  crushed
400 g (13 oz) **fat-free
  fromage frais**
2 tablespoons **icing sugar** or
  artificial sweetener

Reserving a few raspberries for decoration, combine all
the ingredients in a bowl. Spoon into 4 serving dishes.

Serve immediately, decorated with the reserved
raspberries.

For Eton mess, use 4 meringue nests and 300 g
(10 oz) strawberries. Hull and halve or quarter the
strawberries, then add them to the fromage frais with
the sugar or sweetener. Break the meringues into
chunks and fold them through the fromage frais, then
pile into glasses and serve. **Calories per serving 143**

frozen fruity yogurt

Calories per serving **194**
Serves **4**
Preparation time **15 minutes**,
  plus freezing

300 g (10 oz) fresh or frozen
  raspberries
3 **nectarines**, skinned, stoned
  and chopped
2 tablespoons **icing sugar**
400 ml (14 fl oz) **Greek yogurt**
200 ml (7 fl oz) **low-fat Greek
  yogurt**

Put half the raspberries and nectarines in a food
processor or blender and process until smooth.

Stir the purée and the rest of the fruit into the remaining
ingredients, then transfer to a freezerproof container and
freeze for 1 hour. Stir well, then return to the freezer and
freeze until solid.

Serve the frozen yogurt in scoops, as you would ice
cream. It will keep for up to 1 month in the freezer.

For frozen strawberry yogurt, gently cook 250 g
(8 oz) hulled and chopped strawberries in 2 tablespoons
red grape juice. Strain and stir the juice into 1 tablespoon
crème de cassis, 2 tablespoons icing sugar and 300 ml
(½ pint) natural yogurt, then transfer to a freezerproof
container. Continue as above. **Calories per serving 140**

strawberries & meringue

Calories per serving **197**
Serves **4**
Preparation time **15 minutes**
Cooking time **2½ hours**

3 **egg whites**
150 g (5 oz) **light muscovado sugar**
3 teaspoons **cornflour**
1 teaspoon **white vinegar**
1 teaspoon **vanilla extract**
250 g (8 oz) **strawberries**, hulled and sliced

Line 4 tart tins or ramekins with nonstick baking paper. Beat the egg whites until they form stiff peaks, then beat in the sugar, a spoonful at a time, making sure the sugar is incorporated between additions.

Fold in the cornflour, vinegar and vanilla extract.

Spoon the mixture into the tart tins or ramekins and cook in a preheated oven, 120°C (250°F), Gas Mark ½, for 2½ hours.

Place the strawberries in an ovenproof dish and bake with the meringues for the last hour of the cooking time.

Spoon the strawberries and any cooking juices over the meringues to serve.

For baked nectarines with orange meringues, add the grated rind of 1 orange to the meringue with the cornflour. Cut 2 peeled and stoned nectarines into thin slices and place in an ovenproof dish. Sprinkle with 2 tablespoons sugar and 1 tablespoon orange juice, then bake for 45 minutes with the meringues. Serve the fruit on the meringues. **Calories per serving 233**

recipes
under 300
calories

cherry & cinnamon parfait

Calories per serving **201**

Serves **4**

Preparation time **10 minutes**,
  plus freezing

Cooking time **5 minutes**

350 g (11½ oz) jar **morello
  cherries** in syrup

pinch of **ground cinnamon**

½ teaspoon **vanilla extract**

1 tablespoon **caster sugar**

1 **egg yolk**

150 g (5 oz) **half-fat crème
  fraîche**

4 **meringue nests**, broken into
  pieces

fresh cherries, to decorate

Drain the cherries and put 100 ml (3½ fl oz) of the
syrup into a small saucepan. Stir the cinnamon, vanilla
extract and sugar into the syrup and heat for 5 minutes
or until the sugar has dissolved. Set aside to cool.

Stir the egg yolk through the crème fraîche. Add the
drained cherries to the syrup, then mix in the crème
fraîche. Fold the meringue nests carefully through the
mixture.

Transfer to a 300 ml (½ pint) freezerproof container
and freeze for at least 4 hours. Eat within a day, when
the parfait will be softly frozen. Decorate with fresh
cherries before serving.

For pineapple parfait, omit the morello cherries and
instead drain and chop a 400 g (13 oz) can sliced
pineapple, adding to the syrup as above. Omit the egg
yolk, and combine the pineapple, syrup and crème
fraîche. Fold through the meringue nests. **Calories per
serving 180**

sticky toffee & date squares

Calories per serving **201**
Makes **24** squares
Preparation time **25 minutes**,
  plus cooling
Cooking time **55 minutes**

200 g (7 oz) **lightly salted
  butter,** softened, plus extra
  for greasing
225 g (7½ oz) **stoned dates,**
  chopped
150 ml (¼ pint) **water**
150 ml (¼ pint) **double cream**
175 g (6 oz) **light muscovado
  sugar**
100 g (3½ oz) **caster sugar**
2 teaspoons **vanilla bean
  paste**
3 **eggs**
175 g (6 oz) **self-raising flour**
½ teaspoon **baking powder**

Grease a 28 x 18 cm (11 x 7 inch) shallow baking tin and line with nonstick baking paper. Put 125 g (4 oz) of the dates in a saucepan with the measured water and bring to the boil. Reduce the heat and cook gently for 5 minutes or until the dates are pulpy. Turn into a bowl and leave to cool. Put the cream, muscovado sugar and 75 g (3 oz) of the butter in a small saucepan and heat gently until the sugar dissolves. Bring to the boil and boil for 5 minutes or until thickened and caramelized. Leave to cool.

Put the remaining butter in a bowl with the caster sugar, vanilla bean paste and eggs, sift in the flour and baking powder and beat with a hand-held electric whisk until pale and creamy. Beat in the cooked dates and 100 ml (3½ fl oz) of the caramel mixture. Turn into the tin and level the surface. Scatter with the remaining dates.

Bake in a preheated oven, 180°C (350°F), Gas Mark 4, for 25 minutes, or until just firm. Spoon the remaining caramel on top and return to the oven for 15 minutes until the caramel has firmed. Transfer to a wire rack.

For cider-glazed apple slice, grease the tin as above. Put 175 g (6 oz) softened butter, 175 g (6 oz) golden caster sugar, 200 g (7 oz) sifted self-raising flour, ½ teaspoon baking powder, 1 teaspoon ground mixed spice and 3 eggs in a bowl and beat with a hand-held electric whisk until smooth and creamy. Stir in 65 g (2½ oz) sultanas and spread in the tin. Core and slice 2 small red apples and scatter over the surface. Bake as above for 40 minutes or until just firm. Put 100 ml (3½ fl oz) cider in a saucepan and heat until reduced to about 1 tablespoon. Cool and mix with 75 g (3 oz) sifted golden icing sugar until smooth. Drizzle over the cake. **Calories per serving 150**

mango & passion fruit brûlée

Calories per serving **202**
Serves **4**
Preparation time **10 minutes**,
  plus chilling
Cooking time **2 minutes**

1 **small mango**, peeled,
  stoned and thinly sliced
2 **passion fruit**, flesh scooped
  out
300 g (10 oz) **low-fat natural
  yogurt**
200 g (7 oz) **half-fat crème
  fraîche**
1 tablespoon **icing sugar**
few drops **vanilla extract**
2 tablespoons **demerara
  sugar**

Arrange the mango slices in 4 ramekins.

Stir together the passion fruit flesh, yogurt, crème fraîche, icing sugar and vanilla extract in a bowl, then spoon the mixture over the mango. Tap each ramekin to level the surface.

Sprinkle over the demerara sugar and cook the brûlées under a preheated hot grill for 1–2 minutes until the sugar has melted. Chill for about 30 minutes, then serve.

For plum & peach brûlée, replace the mango with 2 sliced peaches. Continue as above, replacing the passion fruit with 4 firm but ripe chopped plums. Before grilling, top each ramekin with a piece of chopped crystallized ginger. **Calories per serving 192**

chocolate brownies

Calories per serving **204**
Makes **9**
Preparation time **10 minutes**
Cooking time **30 minutes**

125 g (4 oz) **reduced-fat
  sunflower spread**
2 **eggs**
125 g (4 oz) **light soft brown
  sugar**
75 g (3 oz) **self-raising flour**
50 g (2 oz) **cocoa**, sieved, plus
  extra to decorate
50 g (2 oz) **plain dark
  chocolate**, chopped
1 teaspoon **chocolate extract**
salt

Grease and line an 18 cm (7 inch) square deep cake tin.

Beat together the sunflower spread, eggs and sugar. Stir in the flour and cocoa, then add the chocolate and chocolate extract. Stir in 1 teaspoon boiling water and a pinch of salt.

Transfer the mixture to the prepared tin and bake in a preheated oven, 190°C (375°F), Gas Mark 5, for 30 minutes or until a skewer comes out clean when inserted in the centre. Leave to cool in the tin, then cut into 9 squares. Dust with a little cocoa powder to serve.

For rum & raisin sauce, to go with the brownies, gently heat 300 ml (½ pint) milk in a saucepan with 2 tablespoons cornflour, 4 tablespoons rum and 4 tablespoons raisins. Add 2 tablespoons sugar to taste, before pouring the sauce over the cooled brownies.
Calories per serving 54

strawberry & lavender crush

Calories per serving **208**
Serves **6**
Preparation time **10 minutes**

400 g (13 oz) **fresh
strawberries**
2 tablespoons **icing sugar**,
plus extra for dusting
4–5 **lavender flower stems**,
plus extra to decorate
400 g (13 oz) **Greek-style
full-fat yogurt**
6 ready-made **meringue
nests**

Reserve 4 small strawberries for decoration. Hull the remainder, put in a bowl with the icing sugar and mash together with a fork. Alternatively, process the strawberries and icing sugar in a food processor or blender to a smooth purée. Pull off the lavender flowers from the stems and crumble them into the purée to taste.

Put the yogurt in a bowl, crumble in the meringues, then lightly mix together. Add the strawberry purée and fold together with a spoon until marbled. Spoon into 4 dessert glasses.

Cut the reserved strawberries in half, then use together with the lavender flowers to decorate the desserts. Lightly dust with icing sugar and serve immediately.

For peach & rose water crush, peel, halve and stone 3 peaches, then roughly chop and mash or process in a food processor or blender with 2 tablespoons clear honey and 2 teaspoons rose water. Continue with the recipe as above, but decorate the desserts with crystallized rose petals. **Calories per serving 227**

banoffee mousse

Calories per serving **209**
Serves **4**
Preparation time **10 minutes**,
  plus setting

2 **gelatine leaves**
3 tablespoons **dulce de leche**
  or **toffee sauce**
125 g (4 oz) **half-fat crème
  fraîche**
65 g (2½ oz) **honey-dipped
  banana chips**
4 **egg whites**

Soften the gelatine in cold water for 2 minutes.

Put the toffee sauce in a small saucepan over gentle heat and stir in the gelatine until it has dissolved.

Stir the toffee mixture into the crème fraîche. Chop the dried banana chips, reserving a few whole ones for decoration, and add to the toffee mixture. Meanwhile, beat the egg whites until stiff, then fold through the toffee and banana mixture. Spoon into 4 glasses and decorate with the reserved banana chips and an extra dollop of toffee sauce, if you like.

For banana & hazelnut toffee creams, mash 2 fresh bananas and mix with the toffee sauce and crème fraîche, omitting the gelatine and egg whites. Serve topped with 50 g (2 oz) chopped toasted hazelnuts. **Calories per serving 235**

chocolate & nectarine cake

Calories per serving **209**
Serves **6**
Preparation time **15 minutes**
Cooking time **45 minutes**

3 **nectarines**
75 g (3 oz) **plain dark chocolate**, chopped
25 g (1 oz) **unsalted butter**
2 **egg yolks**
75 g (3 oz) **caster sugar**
½ teaspoon **chocolate extract**
4 **egg whites**
cocoa powder, for dusting

Grease a 25 cm (10 inch) cake tin and line with baking paper. Put the nectarines in a bowl and pour over boiling water. Leave to stand for 1 minute, then peel off the skins. Halve the nectarines and remove the stones. Drain them well on kitchen paper and arrange, cut side down, in the prepared cake tin.

Put the chocolate and butter in a heatproof bowl and melt together over a pan of simmering water.

Beat together the egg yolks and sugar until the whisk leaves a trail when lifted. The mix should be very pale and quite stiff. Stir in the melted chocolate mixture and chocolate extract.

Beat the egg whites until softly peaking. Stir a spoonful into the cake mix, then fold in the remainder. Spoon the mixture over the nectarines.

Bake the cake in a preheated oven, 180°C (350°F), Gas Mark 4, for 45 minutes or until a skewer inserted comes out clean. Serve warm or cold, dusted with cocoa powder.

For pear & chocolate soufflé cake, make a syrup by bringing 125 g (4 oz) sugar to the boil in 250 ml (8 fl oz) water. Peel 3 pears and poach them in the syrup for 30 minutes at a gentle simmer. Drain the pears, reserving the syrup, then halve, core and drain well. Use these instead of the nectarines in the cake as described above. Add the grated rind of 1 orange to the syrup and boil for 2 minutes, then serve with the cake. **Calories per serving 249**

baby banana & peach strudels

Calories per serving **212**
Makes **8**
Preparation time **30 minutes**
Cooking time **15–18 minutes**

2 **bananas**, about 175 g
  (6 oz) each with skin on,
  peeled and chopped
2 tablespoons **fresh lemon
  juice**
2 small **ripe peaches**, about
  100 g (3½ oz) each, halved,
  stoned and sliced
100 g (3½ oz) **blueberries**
2 tablespoons **caster sugar**
2 tablespoons **fresh
  breadcrumbs**
½ teaspoon **ground
  cinnamon**
6 **filo pastry sheets**, defrosted
  if frozen
50 g (2 oz) **butter**, melted
sifted **icing sugar**, for dusting

Toss the bananas in the lemon juice, then place in a large bowl with the peach slices and blueberries. Mix the sugar, breadcrumbs and cinnamon in a small bowl, then gently mix with the fruit.

Unfold the pastry sheets and put one in front of you with the longest edge nearest you.

Cut in half to make 2 rectangles, 23 x 25 cm (9 x 10 inches). Put 2 heaped spoonfuls of the fruit mixture on each, then fold in the sides, brush the pastry with a little of the melted butter and roll up like a parcel. Repeat to make 8 mini strudels using 4 sheets of pastry.

Brush the strudels with a little more melted butter. Cut the remaining pastry sheets into wide strips, then wrap them like bandages around the strudels, covering any tears or splits in the pastry. Place on an ungreased baking sheet and brush with the remaining butter.

Bake in a preheated oven, 190°C (375°F), Gas Mark 5, for 15–18 minutes until golden brown and crisp. Leave to cool on the baking sheet, then dust with a little sifted icing sugar and arrange on a serving plate. These are best eaten on the day they are made.

For traditional apple strudels, replace the bananas and peaches with 500 g (1 lb) cored, peeled and sliced cooking apples tossed with 2 tablespoons lemon juice and mixed with 50 g (2 oz) sultanas. Use ground almonds instead of the breadcrumbs and combine with the cinnamon. Increase the quantity of sugar to 50 g (2 oz) and continue the recipe as above. **Calories per serving 232**

very berry muffins

Calories per serving **214**
Makes **12**
Preparation time **15 minutes**
Cooking time **25 minutes**

250 g (8 oz) **plain flour**
4 tablespoons **caster sugar**
1 tablespoon **baking powder**
1 **egg**, beaten
200 ml (7 fl oz) **milk**
50 ml (2 fl oz) **vegetable oil**
200 g (7 oz) **mixed berries**,
    roughly chopped

Mix together all the ingredients, except the berries, to make a smooth dough. Fold in the berries.

Line a 12-hole muffin tray with nonstick paper cases and spoon the mixture into the cases. Bake in a preheated oven, 180°C (350°F), Gas Mark 4, for 25 minutes or until a skewer comes out clean when inserted. Transfer to a wire rack to cool.

For banana & pecan muffins, use 200 g (7 oz) chopped fresh banana instead of the berries, adding 125 g (4 oz) chopped pecan nuts with the bananas. Select firm but ripe bananas. Serve warm, drizzled with maple syrup, if liked. **Calories per serving 337** (not including maple syrup)

lychee & coconut sherbet

Calories per serving **216**
Serves **6**
Preparation time **30 minutes**,
   plus freezing
Cooking time **2–4 minutes**

425 g (14 oz) can **pitted
   lychees** in light syrup
50 g (2 oz) **caster sugar**
400 ml (14 fl oz) can **full-fat
   coconut milk**
grated rind and juice of **1 lime**,
   plus extra pared lime rind, to
   decorate (optional)
chocolate cups (see below),
   to serve (optional)
3 **kiwifruits**, peeled and cut
   into wedges, to decorate

Drain the syrup from the can of lychees into a
saucepan, add the sugar and heat gently until the sugar
has dissolved. Boil for 2 minutes, then take off the heat
and leave to cool.

Purée the lychees in a food processor or liquidizer until
smooth, or rub through a sieve. Mix with the coconut
milk, lime rind and juice. Stir in the sugar syrup when it
is cool.

Pour into a shallow plastic container and freeze for
4 hours or until mushy. Beat with a fork or blend in a
food processor or liquidizer until smooth. Pour back into
the plastic container and freeze for 4 hours or overnight
until solid. (Alternatively, freeze in an electric ice-cream
machine for 20 minutes, then transfer to a plastic box
and freeze until required.)

Allow to soften for 15 minutes at room temperature
before serving, then scoop into dishes or chocolate
cups (see below) and decorate with kiwifruit wedges
and pared lime rind curls, if liked.

For chocolate cups, to serve the sherbet in, melt
150 g (5 oz) plain dark chocolate over a pan of
simmering water, then divide between 4 squares of
nonstick baking paper and spread into rough-shaped
circles about 15 cm (6 inches) in diameter. Drape the
paper over upturned glass tumblers, with the chocolate
uppermost, so that the paper falls in soft folds. Chill until
set, then lift the paper and chocolate off the tumblers,
turn over and carefully ease the paper away. **Calories
per serving 145**

pistachio & chocolate meringues

Calories per serving **217**
Makes **12**
Preparation time **30 minutes**
Cooking time **45–60 minutes**

3 **egg whites**
175 g (6 oz) **caster sugar**
50 g (2 oz) **shelled pistachio nuts**, finely chopped
150 g (5 oz) **plain dark chocolate**, broken into pieces
150 ml (¼ pint) **double cream**

Whisk the egg whites in a large clean bowl until stiff. Gradually whisk in the sugar, a teaspoonful at a time, until it has all been added. Whisk for a few minutes more until the meringue mixture is thick and glossy.

Fold in the pistachios, then spoon heaped teaspoonfuls of the mixture into rough swirly mounds on 2 large baking sheets lined with nonstick baking paper.

Bake in a preheated oven, 110°C (225°F), Gas Mark ¼, for 45–60 minutes or until the meringues are firm and may be easily peeled off the paper. Leave to cool still on the paper.

Melt the chocolate in a heatproof bowl set over a saucepan of gently simmering water. Lift the meringues off the paper and dip the bases into the chocolate. Return to the paper, tilted on their sides and leave in a cool place until the chocolate has hardened.

To serve, whip the cream until just holding its shape then use to sandwich the meringues together in pairs. Arrange in paper cake cases, if liked, on a cake plate or stand. Eat on the day they are filled. (Left plain, the meringues will keep for 2–3 days.)

For saffron & chocolate meringues, add a large pinch of saffron threads to the egg whites when first whisking them and omit the pistachios. Dip the meringues in the melted chocolate, fill with the whipped cream and serve as above. **Calories per serving 192**

mango & kiwi upside down cakes

Calories per serving **218**
Cuts into **18**
Preparation time **30 minutes**
Cooking time **30–35 minutes**

1 large **mango**
4 tablespoons **apricot jam**
grated rind and juice of 2
 limes
2 **kiwifruit**, sliced
250 g (8 oz) **soft margarine**
125 g (4 oz) **caster sugar**
125 g (4 oz) light **muscovado
 sugar**
250 g (8 oz) **self-raising flour**
4 **eggs**

Cut a thick slice off each side of the mango to reveal the large flat central stone. Cut the flesh away from the stone, then peel and slice.

Mix the apricot jam with the juice of 1 of the limes, then spoon into the base of an 18 x 28 cm (7 x 11 inch) roasting tin lined with nonstick baking paper. Arrange the mango and kiwifruit randomly over the top.

Put the lime rind and the rest of the juice in a mixing bowl or a food processor, add the remaining ingredients and beat until smooth. Spoon over the top of the fruit and spread the surface level. Bake in a preheated oven, 180°C (350°F), Gas Mark 4, for 30–35 minutes until the cake is well risen, golden and springs back when gently pressed with a fingertip.

Leave to cool in the tin for 10 minutes, then invert the tin on to a wire rack, remove the tin and lining paper and leave to cool completely. Cut into 18 pieces and serve warm with whipped cream. This is best eaten on the day it is made.

For apricot & cranberry upside down cakes, spoon cranberry sauce over the base of the tin instead of the apricot jam. Cover with a 425 g (14 oz) can apricot halves, drained and arranged in rows, instead of the fresh fruit. Replace the lime rind and juice from the cake mixture with the grated rind of 1 orange. Top the fruit with the cake mixture and bake as above. **Calories per serving 208**

very berry & fromage frais fool

Calories per serving **219**
Serves **4**
Preparation time **5 minutes**,
  plus cooling and chilling
Cooking time **about
  5 minutes**

3 tablespoons **crème de
  cassis** or **spiced red fruit
  cordial**
250 g (8 oz) **mixed frozen
  berries**
2–4 tablespoons **icing sugar**,
  to taste
500 g (1 lb) **fat-free fromage
  frais**
250 g (8 oz) **low-fat
  blackcurrant yogurt**
1 **vanilla pod**, split in half
  lengthways
toasted **flaked almonds**, to
  serve

Put the crème de cassis or cordial in a saucepan over a low heat and gently heat, then add the berries. Stir, cover and cook for about 5 minutes or until the fruit has thawed and is beginning to collapse. Remove from the heat and stir in 1–3 tablespoons of the icing sugar, according to taste. Cool completely, then chill for at least 1 hour.

Mix together the fromage frais, yogurt and 1 tablespoon of the icing sugar in a bowl. Scrape in the seeds from the vanilla pod and beat to combine.

Fold the berries into the fromage frais mixture until just combined. Carefully spoon into decorative glasses or glass serving dishes and serve immediately, scattered with toasted almonds, if liked.

For exotic fruit fool, replace the crème de cassis with 3 tablespoons coconut cream and the mixed berries with 250 g (8 oz) exotic fruit mix and add 1 tablespoon lime juice. Heat as above, then blend in a food processor or blender until smooth. Chill as above. Mix the fromage frais with 2 tablespoons coconut cream and 250 g (8 oz) fat-free mango yogurt instead of the blackcurrant yogurt. Fold in the fruit purée and serve sprinkled with toasted coconut flakes. **Calories per serving 262**

griddled bananas with blueberries

Calories per serving **220**
Serves **4**
Preparation time **5 minutes**
Cooking time **8–10 minutes**

4 **bananas**, unpeeled
8 tablespoons **fat-free Greek yogurt**
4 tablespoons **oatmeal** or **fine porridge oats**
125 g (4 oz) **blueberries**
runny honey, to serve

Heat a ridged griddle pan over a medium-hot heat, add the bananas and griddle for 8–10 minutes, or until the skins are beginning to blacken, turning occasionally.

Transfer the bananas to serving dishes and, using a sharp knife, cut open lengthways. Spoon over the yogurt and sprinkle with the oatmeal or oats and blueberries. Serve immediately, drizzled with 1 teaspoon honey per banana.

For oatmeal, ginger & sultana yogurt, mix ½ teaspoon ground ginger with the yogurt in a bowl. Sprinkle with 2–4 tablespoons soft dark brown sugar, according to taste, the oatmeal and 4 tablespoons sultanas. Leave to stand for 5 minutes before serving. **Calories per serving 208**

gluten-free banoffee bites

Calories per serving **222**
Makes **10**
Preparation time **10 minutes**,
  plus cooling
Cooking time **12 minutes**

200 g (7 oz) **brown rice flour**
75 g (3 oz) **lightly salted
  butter**, softened
75 g (3 oz) **golden caster
  sugar**
2 teaspoons **gluten-free
  baking powder**
1 **large banana**, mashed
2 **eggs**
6 **toffees**, chopped
1 tablespoon **light
  muscovado sugar**
15 g (½ oz) **chewy banana
  slices** or **dried banana
  chips**, to decorate

Line a 12-hole muffin tray with paper cases.

Place the flour, butter, caster sugar, baking powder, banana and eggs in a bowl and beat with a hand-held electric whisk until smooth. Stir in the toffees. Divide among the cases and sprinkle over most of the muscovado sugar.

Bake in a preheated oven, 200°C (400°F), Gas Mark 6, for 10–12 minutes until just firm. Remove the cakes from the oven and transfer to a wire rack to cool.

Top with chewy banana slices or banana chips and sprinkle with the remaining sugar.

For walnut & muscovado butterflies, make the muffin mixture as above, replacing the toffees with 50 g (2 oz) finely chopped walnuts. Bake as above and leave to cool. Thoroughly beat 100 g (3½ oz) softened unsalted butter in a bowl with 125 g (4 oz) light muscovado sugar until smooth, pale and creamy. Cut a round from the centre top of each cake using a small sharp knife. Cut each round in half. Spoon or pipe the buttercream into the centres and position the halved rounds to resemble butterfly wings. Dust lightly with icing sugar. **Calories per serving 353**

banoffee meringues

Calories per serving **224**
Makes **8**
Preparation time **30 minutes**
Cooking time **1–1¼ hours**

3 **egg whites**
100 g (3½ oz) **light
  muscovado sugar**
75 g (3 oz) **caster sugar**

To decorate
1 **small ripe banana**
1 tablespoon **lemon juice**
150 ml (¼ pint) **double cream**
8 tablespoons ready-made
  **toffee fudge ice cream
  sauce**

Whisk the egg whites in a large clean bowl until stiff. Gradually whisk in the sugars, a teaspoonful at a time, until it has all been added. Whisk for a few minutes more until the meringue mixture is thick and glossy.

Using a dessertspoon, take a large scoop of meringue mixture, then scoop off the first spoon using a second spoon and drop on to a large baking sheet lined with nonstick baking paper to make an oval-shaped meringue. Continue until all the mixture has been used.

Bake in a preheated oven, 110°C (225°F), Gas Mark ¼, for 1–1¼ hours or until the meringues are firm and easy to peel off the paper. Leave on the paper to cool.

To serve, roughly mash the banana with the lemon juice. Whip the cream until it forms soft swirls, then whisk in 2 tablespoons of the toffee fudge sauce. Combine with the mashed banana, then use to sandwich the meringues together in pairs and arrange in paper cake cases. Drizzle with the remaining toffee fudge sauce and serve immediately. Unfilled meringues may be stored in an airtight tin for up to 3 days.

For coffee toffee meringues, make the meringues as above. To make the filling, whip the cream, then stir in 1–2 teaspoons instant coffee, dissolved in 1 teaspoon boiling water. Use to sandwich the meringues together in pairs. Drizzle toffee fudge sauce over the top of the meringues. **Calories per serving 209**

apricot tea bread

Calories per serving **230**
Cuts into **10**
Preparation time **25 minutes**,
    plus soaking
Cooking time **1 hour**

100 g (3½ oz) ready-to-eat
    dried apricots, chopped
100 g (3½ oz) **sultanas**
100 g (3½ oz) **raisins**
150 g (5 oz) **caster sugar**
300 ml (½ pint) **hot strong
    tea**
275 g (9 oz) **self-raising flour**
1 teaspoon **bicarbonate of
    soda**
1 teaspoon **ground cinnamon**
1 **egg**, beaten

Put the dried fruits and sugar in a mixing bowl, add
the hot tea and mix together. Leave to soak for 4 hours
or overnight.

Mix the flour, bicarbonate of soda and cinnamon
together, add to the soaked fruit with the beaten egg
and mix together well.

Spoon into a greased 1 kg (2 lb) loaf tin, its base and
2 long sides also lined with oiled greaseproof paper.
Spread the surface level, then bake in the centre of
a preheated oven, 160°C (325°F), Gas Mark 3, for
about 1 hour until well risen, the top has cracked and
a skewer inserted into the centre comes out clean.

Leave to cool in the tin for 10 minutes, then loosen
the edges and lift out of the tin using the lining paper.
Transfer to a wire rack, peel off the lining paper and
leave to cool completely. Cut into slices and spread with
a little butter to serve. Store, unbuttered, in an airtight
tin for up to 1 week.

For prune & orange bread, use 175 g (6 oz) chopped
ready-to-eat stoned prunes instead of the apricots and
sultanas, and increase the quantity of raisins to 125 g
(4 oz). Mix with the caster sugar as above, add the
grated rind of 1 orange, then soak in 150 ml (¼ pint)
orange juice and 150 ml (¼ pint) boiling water instead
of the tea. Add the flour, bicarbonate of soda and
beaten egg as above, omitting the cinnamon. Spoon into
a loaf tin and continue the recipe as above. **Calories
per serving 227**

summer fruit crunch

Calories per serving **231**
Serves **4**
Preparation time **10 minutes**
Cooking time **20 minutes**

50 g (2 oz) **rolled oats**
½ teaspoon **ground
  cinnamon**
½ teaspoon **mixed spice**
pinch of **ground ginger**
15 g (½ oz) **butter**, melted
1 tablespoon **clear honey**
2 tablespoons **sultanas**
400 g (13 oz) mixed fresh or
  frozen **summer fruits**
50 g (2 oz) **icing sugar**, plus
  extra to garnish
2 tablespoons **crème de
  cassis**
½ teaspoon **vanilla extract**
1 tablespoon **flaked almonds**,
  toasted, to garnish

Mix the oats and spices with the melted butter and honey until well combined.

Press on to a baking sheet and cook in a preheated oven, 180°C (350°F), Gas Mark 4, for 20 minutes, turning once. Remove and leave to cool before mixing in the sultanas.

Meanwhile, put the summer fruits in a pan with the icing sugar and 1 tablespoon water. Warm over a medium-low heat, stirring occasionally, until the fruit begins to collapse. Remove from the heat and stir in the crème de cassis and vanilla extract.

Spoon the fruit into dishes and sprinkle over the crunchy topping. Garnish with the toasted almonds and a sprinkling of icing sugar. Serve immediately.

For autumn plum crunch, stone and quarter 500 g (1 lb) plums and use instead of the summer fruits. Cook the plums in 100 ml (3½ fl oz) apple juice until just tender. Substitute the crème de cassis for sloe gin. Spoon into the dishes and finish as above. **Calories per serving 236**

blueberry & lemon ice cream

Calories per serving **234**
Serves **4**
Preparation time **10 minutes**,
    plus freezing

500 g (1 lb) **frozen
    blueberries**
500 g (1 lb) **fat-free Greek
    yogurt**
125 g (4 oz) **icing sugar**, plus
    extra to decorate
grated rind of 2 **lemons**
1 tablespoon **lemon juice**

Reserve a few blueberries for decoration. Put the remainder of the blueberries in a food processor or blender with the yogurt, icing sugar and lemon rind and juice and process until smooth.

Spoon the mixture into a 600 ml (1 pint) freezerproof container and freeze.

Eat when the frozen yogurt is softly frozen and easily spoonable. Before serving, decorate with the reserved blueberries and a sprinkling of icing sugar. Use within 3 days.

For peach & blackcurrant ice cream waffles, lightly toast 4 waffles, then top each with a sliced canned peach and drizzle with honey. Serve with blackcurrant and lemon ice cream. Use 500 g (1 lb) frozen blackcurrants in place of the blueberries. The same quantity of frozen blackberries or raspberries can also be used. **Calories per serving 366**

sweet carrot & rosemary scones

Calories per serving **236**
Makes **12**
Preparation time **15 minutes**
Cooking time **8–10 minutes**

225 g (7½ oz) **stoneground spelt flour**
2 teaspoons **baking powder**
½ teaspoon **cream of tartar**
2 teaspoons **fresh rosemary**, finely chopped
2 tablespoons **caster sugar**
50 g (2 oz) **slightly salted butter**, chilled and diced
125 g (4 oz) **small carrots**, finely grated
100 ml (3½ fl oz) **milk**, plus extra to glaze

To serve
mascarpone cheese
fruit jelly, such as crab apple, apple or orange

Sift the flour, baking powder and cream of tartar into a bowl or food processor, tipping in the grains left in the sieve. Stir in the rosemary and sugar. Add the butter and rub in with the fingertips or process until the mixture resembles breadcrumbs. Stir in the grated carrots and milk and mix or blend briefly to a soft dough, adding a dash more milk if the dough feels dry.

Knead the dough on a lightly floured surface until smooth, then roll out to 1.5 cm (¾ inch) thick. Cut out 22–24 rounds using a 3 cm (1¼ inch) plain biscuit cutter, re-rolling the trimmings to make more. Place slightly apart on a greased baking sheet and brush with milk.

Bake in a preheated oven, 220°C (425°F), Gas Mark 7, for 8–10 minutes until risen and pale golden. Transfer to a wire rack to cool.

Split the scones and serve spread with mascarpone and fruit jelly.

For wholemeal apple & sultana scones, mix 125 g (4 oz) plain wholemeal flour, 100 g (3½ oz) self-raising flour, 1 teaspoon ground mixed spice and 2 teaspoons baking powder in a bowl or food processor. Add 40 g (1½ oz) slightly salted butter, chilled and diced, and rub in with the fingertips or process until the mixture resembles breadcrumbs. Stir or blend in 50 g (2 oz) chopped sultanas and 1 peeled, cored and grated dessert apple. Add 125 ml (4 fl oz) milk and mix or blend to a soft dough, adding a little more milk if the dough feels dry. Roll out, shape and bake as above. Calories per serving 102

chocolate yum yums

Calories per serving **240**
Cuts into **12**
Preparation time **15 minutes**,
   plus chilling

150 g (5 oz) **plain dark
   chocolate**, broken into
   pieces
100 g (3½ oz) **crunchy
   peanut butter**
25 g (1 oz) **butter**
2 tablespoons **golden syrup**
150 g (5 oz) **digestive
   biscuits**
50 g (2 oz) **almonds** or
   cashew nuts
sugared almonds, roughly
   chopped, to decorate

Put the chocolate, peanut butter, butter and syrup in a saucepan and heat gently until melted, stirring occasionally. Remove from the heat.

Place the biscuits in a plastic bag and crush roughly using a rolling pin. Stir the crushed biscuits and the nuts into the chocolate and stir until evenly coated.

Spoon the mixture into a 20 cm (8 inch) shallow square cake tin lined with nonstick baking paper, and spread the surface level. Chill for 4 hours until firm. Lift the cake out of the tin using the lining paper, cut into 12 small squares and peel off the paper. Decorate with sugared almonds. Store in an airtight tin for up to 3 days.

For chocolate marshmallow wedges, omit the peanut butter, nuts and sugared almonds. Melt the chocolate with 75 g (3 oz) butter and 75 g (3 oz) golden syrup. Cool slightly, then stir in 65 g (2½ oz) roughly chopped sponge fingers, 65 g (2½ oz) roughly chopped glacé cherries and 100 g (3½ oz) mini marshmallows. Spoon into a clingfilm-lined 20 cm (8 inch) round tin and sprinkle the top with 25 g (1 oz) halved mini marshmallows. Chill as above. Remove from the tin, peel off the clingfilm and cut into thin wedges. **Calories per serving 200**

chocolate cornflake bars

Calories per serving **240**
Makes **12**
Preparation time **10 minutes**,
    plus chilling
Cooking time **3 minutes**

200 g (7 oz) **milk chocolate**,
    broken into pieces
2 tablespoons **golden syrup**
50 g (2 oz) **olive oil spread**
125 g (4 oz) **cornflakes**

Melt the chocolate with the golden syrup and olive oil spread in a bowl over a pan of simmering water.

Stir in the cornflakes and mix well together.

Grease a 28 x 18 cm (11 x 7 inch) tin. Turn the mixture into the tin, chill until set, then cut into 12 bars.

For crunchy muesli & apricot cakes, replace the cornflakes with 125 g (4 oz) muesli and 50 g (2 oz) chopped dried apricots. Combine with the chocolate mixture, spoon into 12 paper cake cases and chill until set. **Calories per serving 247**

st clement's cheesecake

Calories per serving **245**
Serves **10**
Preparation time **10 minutes**,
  plus cooling and chilling
Cooking time **50 minutes**

50 g (2 oz) **unsalted butter**
175 g (6 oz) **low-fat oat**
  biscuits, crushed
2 x 250 g (8 oz) tubs **quark**
125 g (4 oz) **caster sugar**
2 **eggs**
grated rind and juice of 2
  oranges
grated rind and juice of 1
  lemon
75 g (3 oz) **sultanas**
juliennes of orange and
  lemon rind, to decorate

Lightly grease a 20 cm (8 inch) nonstick, loose-based round cake tin.

Melt the butter in a saucepan, stir in the biscuit crumbs, then press them over the base and sides of the cake tin. Bake in a preheated oven, 150°C (300°F), Gas Mark 2, for 10 minutes.

Beat together the remaining ingredients in a bowl, spoon the mixture into the cake tin and bake for 40 minutes until just firm. Turn off the oven and leave the cheesecake to cool in the oven for an hour.

Transfer the cheesecake to the refrigerator for 2 hours, then serve decorated with juliennes of orange and lemon rind.

For lime & raspberry cheesecake, replace the oranges, lemon and sultanas with 2–3 drops vanilla extract and the grated rind and juice of 1 lime, then cook as above. Once chilled, decorate with 125 g (4 oz) raspberries. **Calories per serving 221**

cidered apple & fig loaf

Calories per serving **246**

Cuts into **10**

Preparation time **20 minutes**,
plus soaking

Cooking time **1 hour–1 hour
10 minutes**

300 ml (½ pint) **dry cider**

1 **large cooking apple**, about
300 g (10 oz) in total, cored,
peeled and chopped

175 g (6 oz) **ready-to-eat
dried figs**, chopped

150 g (5 oz) **caster sugar**

300 g (10 oz) **self-raising
flour**

2 **eggs**, beaten

1 tablespoon **sunflower
seeds**

1 tablespoon **pumpkin seeds**

Pour the cider into a saucepan, add the apple and figs
and bring to the boil. Simmer for 3–5 minutes until the
apples are just tender but still firm. Remove the pan
from the heat and leave to soak for 4 hours.

Mix the sugar, flour and eggs into the soaked fruit and
stir well.

Spoon into a greased 1 kg (2 lb) loaf tin, its base and
2 long sides also lined with oiled greaseproof paper, and
spread the surface level. Sprinkle with the seeds and
bake in the centre of a preheated oven, 160°C (325°F),
Gas Mark 3, for 1 hour–1 hour 10 minutes until well
risen, the top has slightly cracked and a skewer inserted
into the centre comes out clean.

Leave to cool in the tin for 10 minutes, then loosen
the edges and lift out of the tin using the lining paper.
Transfer to a wire rack, peel off the lining paper and
leave to cool completely. Serve cut into slices and
spread with a little butter. Store in an airtight tin for
up to 1 week.

For apple & mixed fruit loaf, cook the apple as above
in 300 ml (½ pint) apple juice instead of cider with 175 g
(6 oz) luxury mixed dried fruit instead of dried figs.
Continue as above, spooning the mixture into the tin
and sprinkling the top with roughly crushed sugar lumps
or leaving plain if preferred. **Calories per serving 252**

caramelized blueberry custards

Calories per serving **251**
Serves **6**
Preparation time **10 minutes**,
plus cooling
Cooking time **5 minutes**

150 g (5 oz) **granulated
sugar**
3 tablespoons **cold water**
2 tablespoons **boiling water**
150 g (5 oz) fresh (not frozen)
blueberries
400 g (13 oz) **fromage frais**
425 g (14 oz) can or carton
custard

Put the sugar and measured cold water into a frying pan and heat gently, stirring very occasionally, until the sugar has completely dissolved. Bring to the boil, then cook for 3–4 minutes, without stirring, until the syrup is just changing colour and is golden around the edges.

Add the measured boiling water, standing well back as the syrup will spit, then tilt the pan to mix. Add the blueberries and cook for 1 minute. Remove the pan from the heat and leave to cool slightly.

Mix the fromage frais and custard together, spoon into 6 small dishes, then spoon the blueberry mixture over the top. Serve immediately, with baby meringues, if liked.

For banana custards, make the caramel as above, then add 2 sliced bananas instead of the blueberries. Cool slightly, then spoon over the custard and fromage frais mixture. Decorate with grated plain dark chocolate. **Calories per serving 286**

mini christmas cakes

Calories per serving **253**
Makes **12**
Preparation time **40 minutes**,
  plus cooling
Cooking time **15 minutes**

50 g (2 oz) **lightly salted
  butter**, softened
50 g (2 oz) **dark muscovado
  sugar**
1 **egg**
65 g (2½ oz) **self-raising
  flour**
½ teaspoon **ground mixed
  spice**
¼ teaspoon **baking powder**
65 g (2½ oz) **mixed dried
  fruit**
15 g (½ oz) **Brazil nuts**,
  chopped
2 tablespoons **brandy** or
  orange-flavoured liqueur
2 tablespoons **smooth apricot
  jam**
1 teaspoon **hot water**
250 g (8 oz) **marzipan**
icing sugar, for dusting
150 g (5 oz) **royal icing
  sugar**, sifted
edible silver balls, to
  decorate

Place 12 mini silicone muffin cases on a baking sheet.

Put the butter, sugar and egg in a bowl, sift in the flour, mixed spice and baking powder and beat with a hand-held electric whisk until light and creamy. Beat in the dried fruit and nuts. Divide among the cases.

Bake in a preheated oven, 180°C (350°F), Gas Mark 4, for 15 minutes, or until risen and just firm. Leave in the cases for 2 minutes, then transfer to a wire rack to cool completely.

Using a skewer or cocktail stick, pierce holes over the tops of the cakes and spoon over the brandy or orange liqueur. Store in an airtight container for up to 1 week.

Mix the apricot jam with the measured hot water and brush over the tops of the cakes. Thinly roll out the marzipan on a surface dusted with icing sugar and cut out 4 cm (1¾ inch) rounds using a small cutter, re-rolling the trimmings to make more. Press onto the tops of the cakes.

Beat the royal icing sugar in a bowl with enough cold water to make a softly peaking consistency. Swirl a little over the cakes and decorate with silver balls.

For Christmas tree cakes, make the cakes as above and cover with marzipan. Thinly roll out 100 g (3½ oz) green ready-to-roll icing on a surface dusted with icing sugar and cut out 16 simple Christmas tree shapes using a small cutter. Transfer to a tray lined with baking paper for 2–3 hours to firm up. Spread the cakes with royal icing as above and gently position a tree on top of each. Decorate with garlands of red writing icing, pushing silver balls into the piping to secure. **Calories per serving 266**

stollen slice

Calories per serving **253**
Makes **15 slices**
Preparation time **30 minutes**,
  plus proving
Cooking time **25 minutes**

40 g (1½ oz) **salted butter**,
  plus extra for greasing
175 g (6 oz) **strong white
  bread flour**, plus extra for
  dusting
1½ teaspoons **fast-action
  dried yeast**
½ teaspoon **ground mixed
  spice**
25 g (1 oz) **caster sugar**
100 ml (3½ fl oz) **warm milk**
75 g (3 oz) **sultanas**
25 g (1 oz) **chopped almonds**
25 g (1 oz) **chopped candied
  peel**
150 g (5 oz) **marzipan**
icing sugar, for dusting

Grease a large loaf tin with a base measurement of about 25 x 10 cm (10 x 4 inches). Put the flour, yeast, mixed spice and sugar in a bowl. Melt 25 g (1 oz) of the butter, mix with the milk and add to the bowl. Mix with a round-bladed knife to make a soft but not sticky dough. Turn out onto a lightly floured surface and knead for 10 minutes until smooth and elastic. (Alternatively, use a freestanding mixer with a dough hook and knead for 5 minutes.) Place in a lightly oiled bowl, cover with clingfilm and leave to rise in a warm place for about 1½ hours or until doubled in size.

Turn the dough out onto a floured surface and knead in the sultanas, almonds and candied peel. Cover loosely with a tea towel and leave to rest for 10 minutes. Roll out the dough on a floured surface to a 25 x 20 cm (10 x 8 inch) rectangle. Roll the marzipan under the palms of your hands to form a log shape about 23 cm (9 inches) long and flatten to about 5 mm (¼ inch) thick. Lay the marzipan down the length of the dough, slightly to one side, and fold the rest of the dough over it. Transfer to the tin and press down gently.

Cover loosely with oiled clingfilm and leave to rise in a warm place for about 30 minutes until slightly risen. Remove the clingfilm. Bake in a preheated oven, 220°C (425°F), Gas Mark 7, for 25 minutes until risen and golden. Leave for 5 minutes, then turn out of the tin, place on a wire rack, cover with a sheet of foil and place a weight on top to keep the stollen compact while cooling. Melt the remaining butter and brush over the bread. Dust generously with icing sugar.

cidered apple jellies

Calories per serving **254**
Preparation time **20 minutes**,
  plus chilling
Cooking time **15 minutes**
Finishing time **5 minutes**
Serves **6**

1 kg (2 lb) **cooking apples**,
  peeled, cored and sliced
300 ml (½ pint) **cider**
150 ml (¼ pint) **water**, plus
  4 tablespoons
75 g (3 oz) **caster sugar**
finely grated rind of 2 **lemons**
4 teaspoons **powdered**
  gelatine
150 ml (¼ pint) **double cream**

Put the apples, cider, 150 ml (¼ pint) of water, sugar and the rind of one of the lemons into a saucepan. Cover and simmer for 15 minutes until the apples are soft.

Meanwhile put the 4 tablespoons of water into a small bowl and sprinkle over the gelatine, making sure that all the powder is absorbed by the water. Set aside.

Add the gelatine to the hot apples and stir until completely dissolved. Purée the apple mixture in a blender or food processor until smooth, then pour into 6 tea cups. Allow to cool, then chill for 4–5 hours until fully set.

When ready to serve, whip the cream until it forms soft peaks. Spoon over the jellies and sprinkle with the remaining lemon rind.

For cidered apple granita, omit the gelatine and pour the puréed apple mixture into a shallow dish so that the mixture is about 2.5 cm (1 inch) deep or less. Freeze for about 2 hours until mushy around the edges, then beat with a fork. Freeze for 2 hours more, beating the granita at 30-minute intervals until the texture of crushed ice. Freeze until ready to serve, then scoop into small glasses. **Calories per serving 250**

tropical ginger cake

Calories per serving **257**
Makes **20** squares
Preparation time **30 minutes**,
 plus cooling
Cooking time **25 minutes**

150 g (5 oz) **butter**, plus extra
 for greasing
125 g (4 oz) **light muscovado
 sugar**
3 tablespoons **golden syrup**
250 g (8 oz) **self-raising flour**
1 teaspoon **baking powder**
3 teaspoons **ground ginger**
50 g (2 oz) **desiccated
 coconut**
3 **eggs**, beaten
200 g (7 oz) **canned
 pineapple rings**, drained
 and chopped

Lime frosting
100 g (3½ oz) **unsalted
 butter**, softened
200 g (7 oz) **icing sugar**,
 sifted
grated rind and juice of **1 lime**

To decorate
ready-to-eat **dried papaya** and
 apricot, diced
dried **coconut shavings**

Grease and line the base of an 18 x 28 cm (7 x 11 inch)
roasting tin with nonstick baking paper. Heat the butter,
sugar and syrup gently in a saucepan, stirring until melted.

Mix the dry ingredients together in a mixing bowl, then
stir in the melted butter mixture and beat together until
smooth. Stir in the eggs, then the chopped pineapple.
Turn into the tin and level the surface.

Bake in a preheated oven, 180°C (350°F), Gas Mark 4,
for about 20 minutes until well risen and firm to touch.
Leave to cool in the tin for 10 minutes, then transfer to
a wire rack.

Make the lime frosting by beating the butter, icing
sugar and half the lime rind and juice together to make
a smooth light mixture. Turn the cake over so the top is
uppermost, then spread with the frosting. Decorate with
a sprinkling of the remaining lime rind, ready-to-eat dried
fruits and coconut shavings. Cut into 20 squares to serve.

For ginger muffin slice, grease and line a 750 g–1 kg
(1½–2 lb) loaf tin with nonstick baking paper. Beat
together 100 g (3½ oz) melted lightly salted butter,
175 ml (6 fl oz) milk and 1 egg. Mix together 250 g (8 oz)
plain flour, 2 teaspoons baking powder, 2 teaspoons
ground ginger, 150 g (5 oz) golden caster sugar, 25 g
(1 oz) oatmeal and 75 g (3 oz) raisins in a bowl. Stir in
the milk mixture until just combined and turn into the tin.
Bake in a preheated oven, 180°C (350°F), Gas Mark 4
for about 45 minutes until risen and just firm. Dust with
caster sugar and serve freshly baked. **Calories per
serving 138**

fig & honey pots

Calories per serving **260**
Serves **4**
Preparation time **10 minutes**,
  plus chilling

6 ripe **fresh figs**, thinly sliced,
  plus 2 extra, cut into wedges,
  to decorate (optional)
450 ml (¾ pint) **full-fat Greek
  yogurt**
4 tablespoons **clear honey**
2 tablespoons **pistachio nuts**,
  chopped

Arrange the fig slices snugly in the bottom of 4 glasses or glass bowls. Spoon the yogurt over the figs and chill in the refrigerator for 10–15 minutes.

Just before serving, drizzle 1 tablespoon honey over each dessert and sprinkle the pistachio nuts on top. Decorate with the wedges of fig, if liked.

For hot figs with honey, heat a griddle pan, add 8 whole ripe fresh figs and cook for 8 minutes, turning occasionally, until charred on the outside. Alternatively, cook under a preheated grill. Remove and cut in half. Divide between 4 plates, top each with 1 heaped tablespoonful of Greek yogurt and drizzle with a little clear honey. **Calories per serving 151**

lime & mango sorbet

Calories per serving **260**
Serves **4**
Preparation time **10 minutes**,
  plus freezing
Cooking time **5 minutes**

150 g (5 oz) **caster sugar**
250 ml (8 fl oz) **water**
250 ml (8 fl oz) **lime juice**
grated rind of **1 lime**
3 **mangoes**, peeled and
  stoned
2 **egg whites**

Line a 2 lb (1 kg) loaf tin with clingfilm or nonstick baking paper. Put the sugar in a saucepan, add 250 ml (8 fl oz) water and warm gently until the sugar is dissolved. Remove from the heat and stir in the lime juice and grated rind.

Meanwhile, process the mango flesh to make a smooth purée, reserving 4 thin slices for the decoration. Stir the purée into the lime syrup and pour the mixture into the loaf tin. Freeze for at least 4 hours or overnight until solid.

Remove the sorbet from the tin and blend or process with the egg whites. Return the mixture to the tin and return to the freezer until firm. Eat within 3 days, because the flavour of fresh fruit sorbet deteriorates quickly and this one has raw egg in it. Before serving, decorate each portion of sorbet with a thin slice of mango and serve with a couple of wafer biscuits.

For passion fruit sorbet, omit the mangoes and use 250 ml (8 fl oz) passion fruit juice instead of the lime juice. The passion fruit juice can be bought or scooped from fresh fruit. To prepare fresh fruit, halve and scoop out the pips and pulp into a sieve. Rub all the juice through the sieve, then discard the seeds. **Calories per serving 175**

poached apricots with pistachios

Calories per serving **260**
Serves **4**
Preparation time **10 minutes**,
   plus chilling and cooling
Cooking time **8 minutes**

125 g (4 oz) **caster sugar**
300 ml (½ pint) **water**
2 strips of **lemon rind**
2 **cardamom pods**
1 **vanilla pod**
12 **apricots**, halved and
   stoned
1 tablespoon **lemon juice**
1 tablespoon **rose water**
25 g (1 oz) **pistachio nuts**,
   finely chopped
vanilla ice cream or **Greek-style yogurt**, to serve
   (optional)

Put a large bowl in the freezer to chill. Put the sugar and measured water in a wide saucepan and heat over a low heat until the sugar has dissolved. Meanwhile, cut the lemon rind into fine strips, crush the cardamom pods and split the vanilla pod in half. Add the lemon rind, cardamom and vanilla pod to the pan.

Add the apricots and simmer gently for 5 minutes, or until softened. Remove from the heat, add the lemon juice and rose water and transfer to the chilled bowl. Leave to cool until required.

Spoon the apricots and a little of the syrup into serving bowls, scatter over the pistachio nuts and serve with ice cream or Greek-style yogurt, if you like.

For poached peaches with almonds, follow the first stage of the recipe above, but replace the lemon rind with orange rind and the cardamom pods with ½ cinnamon stick. Peel, halve and stone 4 large peaches, then poach until softened and add orange juice and orange flower water in place of the lemon juice and rose water. After cooling, serve scattered with toasted flaked almonds instead of the pistachio nuts. **Calories per serving 151**

citrus refresher

calories per serving **274**
Serves **4**
Preparation time **10 minutes**
Cooking time **6–7 minutes**

150 ml (¼ pint) **chilled
    orange juice** from a carton
150 ml (¼ pint) **water**
125 g (4 oz) **caster sugar**
juice of ½ **lemon**
2 **ruby grapefruit**
4 **oranges** (a mix of ordinary
    and blood oranges, if
    available)
1 **orange-fleshed melon**
½ **pomegranate**

Pour the orange juice and measured water into a saucepan, add the sugar and heat gently until the sugar has dissolved, then simmer for 5 minutes until syrupy. Take off the heat and mix in the lemon juice.

Cut a slice off the top and bottom of each grapefruit, then cut away the rest of the peel in downward slices using a small serrated knife. Holding the fruit over a bowl, cut between the membranes to release the segments. Cut a slice off the top and bottom of the oranges, then cut away the rest of the peel. Cut into segments and add to the bowl.

Cut the melon in half, scoop out the seeds, then cut away the peel and dice the flesh. Add to the citrus fruit, then pour over the syrup. Flex the pomegranate to release the seeds, sprinkle over the salad, then chill until ready to serve.

For orange & fig refresher, make the syrup as above. Omit the grapefruit and increase the number of oranges to 6. Cut 4 fresh figs into wedges, peel and add to the oranges. Add the sugar syrup and sprinkle with some fresh mint leaves. Serve chilled. **Calories per serving 278**

roasted pears with oriental spices

Calories per serving **279**

Serves **4**

Preparation time **20 minutes**

Cooking time **25 minutes**

4 **pears**

8 tablespoons **dry** or **sweet sherry**

8 tablespoons **water**

6–8 pieces **star anise**

1 **cinnamon stick**, broken into pieces

8 **cloves**

8 **cardamom pods**, crushed

50 g (2 oz) **unsalted butter**

4 tablespoons **light muscovado sugar**

1 **orange**

Leave the peel on the pears and cut them in half, down through the stems to the base. Scoop out the core, then put in a roasting tin with the cut sides up. Spoon the sherry into the core cavity of each pear and the measured water into the base of the tin. Sprinkle the spices over the pears, including the cardamom pods and their black seeds. Dot with the butter, then sprinkle with the sugar.

Remove the rind from the orange and scatter into the tin. Cut the orange into wedges and squeeze the juice over the pears. Add the wedges to the base of the roasting tin.

Cook in a preheated oven, 180°C (350°F), Gas Mark 4, for 25 minutes until tender and just beginning to brown, spooning the pan juices over the pears halfway through cooking and again at the end.

Spoon into shallow dishes, drizzle with the pan juices and serve with crème fraîche or Greek yogurt.

For roast apples with peppercorns, core and halve 4 dessert apples, then place, cut side up, in a roasting tin. Spoon 200 ml (7 fl oz) cider over the apples and into the roasting tin. Sprinkle with 1 teaspoon coarsely crushed multicoloured peppercorns and 1 broken cinnamon stick. Dot with butter and sprinkle with sugar as above. Remove the rind from 1 lemon and reserve for decoration, then cut the lemon into wedges, squeeze the juice over the apples and add the wedges to the base of the tin. Bake as above. **Calories per serving 251**

blood orange sorbet

Calories per serving **282**
Serves **4**
Preparation time **25 minutes**,
  plus chilling and freezing
Cooking time about **20
  minutes**

250 g (8 oz) **caster sugar**
250 ml (8 fl oz) **water**
pared rind of 2 **blood oranges**
300 ml (½ pint) **blood orange
  juice**
chilled **Campari**, to serve
  (optional)
orange rind, to decorate

Heat the sugar over a low heat in a small saucepan with the measured water, stirring occasionally until completely dissolved.

Add the orange rind and increase the heat. Without stirring, boil the syrup for about 12 minutes, then set aside to cool completely.

When it is cold, strain the sugar syrup over the orange juice and stir together. Refrigerate for about 2 hours until really cold.

Pour the chilled orange syrup into an ice cream machine and churn for about 10 minutes. When the sorbet is almost frozen, scrape it into a plastic container and put it in the freezer compartment for a further hour until completely frozen. Alternatively, pour the chilled orange syrup into a shallow metal container and put it in the freezer for 2 hours. Remove and whisk with a hand-held electric whisk or balloon whisk, breaking up all the ice crystals. Return it to the freezer and repeat this process every hour or so until frozen.

Serve scoops of sorbet with a splash of chilled Campari, if liked, and decorate with thin strips of orange rind.

For papaya & lime sorbet, dissolve 125 g (4 oz) caster sugar in 150 ml (¼ pint) water. Boil for 5 minutes, then set aside to cool. Deseed, peel and dice the flesh of 1 ripe papaya. Process the papaya with the cooled sugar syrup. Stir in the grated rind and juice of 2 limes, chill and proceed as above. **Calories per serving 181**

toffee & chocolate popcorn

Calories per serving **282**
Serves **12**
Preparation time **1 minute**
Cooking time **4 minutes**

120 g (4 oz) **popping corn**
250 g (8 oz) **butter**
250 g (8 oz) **light muscovado sugar**
2 tablespoons **cocoa powder**

Microwave the popping corn in a large bowl with a lid on high (900 watts) for 4 minutes. Alternatively, cook in a pan with a lid on the hob, on a medium heat, for a few minutes until popping.

Meanwhile, gently heat the butter, muscovado sugar and cocoa powder in a pan until the sugar has dissolved and the butter has melted.

Stir the warm popcorn into the mixture and serve.

For toffee, marshmallow & nut popcorn, omit the muscovado sugar and cocoa. Microwave the popping corn as above, then gently heat 150 g (5 oz) chewy toffees, 125 g (4 oz) butter, 125 g (4 oz) marshmallows and 50 g (2 oz) plain chocolate in a pan until melted. Serve as above. **Calories per serving 341**

hot cross buns

Calories per serving **287**
Makes **12**
Preparation time **1 hour**, plus
  standing and rising
Cooking time **20 minutes**

2 tablespoons **active dried
  yeast**
1 teaspoon **sugar**
150 ml (¼ pint) **milk**, warmed
4 tablespoons warm **water**
500 g (1 lb) **strong bread
  flour**
1 teaspoon **salt**
½ teaspoon **ground mixed
  spice**
½ teaspoon **ground
  cinnamon**
½ teaspoon grated **nutmeg**
50 g (2 oz) **caster sugar**
50 g (2 oz) **butter**, melted and
  cooled
1 **egg**, beaten
125 g (4 oz) **currants**
40 g (1½ oz) **chopped mixed
  peel**
75 g (3 oz) ready-made
  shortcrust pastry

For the glaze
3 tablespoons **caster sugar**
4 tablespoons **milk** and **water**

Combine the yeast and sugar with the warmed milk
and water. Stir into 125 g (4 oz) of the flour. Leave in
a warm place for about 20 minutes. Sift the remaining
flour into a bowl. Add the salt, spices and caster sugar.

Add the butter and egg to the yeast mixture. Stir this
into the flour and mix well. Add the dried fruit and mix
to a fairly soft dough. Add a little water if necessary.

Turn out the dough on to a lightly floured surface and
knead well. Place in an oiled plastic bag and allow to
rise for 1–1½ hours at room temperature until doubled
in size. Turn out on to a floured surface and knead with
your knuckles to knock out the air bubbles.

Divide the dough and shape into 12 round buns.
Flatten each slightly, then space well apart on floured
baking sheets. Cover and put in a warm place to rise for
20–30 minutes until doubled in size. Meanwhile, thinly
roll out the pastry and cut it into 24 thin strips about
8 cm (3½ inches) long.

Dampen the strips and lay 2, damp side down, in a
cross over each bun. Bake in a preheated oven, 190°C
(375°F), Gas Mark 5, for 20 minutes or until golden
brown and firm.

Make the glaze. Dissolve the sugar in the milk and
water mixture over a low heat. Brush the cooked buns
twice with the glaze. Serve hot, split and buttered.

For gingered fruit buns, use 125 g (4 oz) luxury dried
fruit instead of the currants, and 2 tablespoons chopped
glacé ginger in place of the mixed peel. Omit the pastry
crosses and glaze as above. **Calories per serving 285**

blueberry bakewell

Calories per serving **289**
Cuts into **18**
Preparation time **20 minutes**
Cooking time **1 hour**

350 g (11½ oz) ready-made
  sweet shortcrust pastry
6 tablespoons **blueberry jam**
  (see below for homemade)
125 g (4 oz) **slightly salted
  butter**, softened
125 g (4 oz) **caster sugar**
2 **eggs**
125 g (4 oz) **self-raising flour**
½ teaspoon **baking powder**
1 teaspoon **almond extract**
100 g (3½ oz) **ground
  almonds**
4 tablespoons **flaked
  almonds**
75 g (3 oz) **icing sugar**, sifted

Roll out the pastry on a lightly floured surface and use to line a greased 28 x 18 cm (11 x 7 inch) shallow baking tin. Line the pastry case with baking parchment and baking beans (or dried beans reserved for the purpose). Bake in a preheated oven, 200°C (400°F), Gas Mark 4, for 15 minutes. Remove the paper and beans and bake for a further 5 minutes. Reduce the oven temperature to 180°C (350°F), Gas Mark 4.

Spread the base of the pastry with the jam. Beat together the butter, caster sugar, eggs, flour, baking powder and almond extract in a bowl until smooth and creamy. Beat in the ground almonds. Spoon the mixture over the jam and spread gently in an even layer.

Scatter with the flaked almonds and bake in the oven for about 40 minutes until risen and just firm to the touch. Leave to cool in the tin.

Beat the icing sugar with a dash of water in a bowl to give the consistency of thin cream. Spread in a thin layer over the cake. Allow to set, then cut into squares or fingers.

For homemade blueberry jam, put 500 g (1 lb) fresh blueberries, 4 tablespoons lemon juice and 2 tablespoons water in a large saucepan and cook gently for about 8–10 minutes until the berries are soft. Stir in 450 g (14½ oz) preserving or granulated sugar and heat gently until the sugar dissolves. Bring to the boil and boil for 10–15 minutes until setting point is reached. Ladle into sterilized jars, cover and label. **Calories per serving 141**

154

mango & passion fruit trifle

Calories per serving **292**
Serves **4**
Preparation time **10 minutes**,
  plus chilling

4 **sponge fingers**
150 g (5 oz) **full-fat Greek
  yogurt**
200 g (7 oz) **crème fraîche**
4 **passion fruit**
1 **mango**, peeled, stoned and
  diced

Break each biscuit into 4 pieces and arrange them in
4 tumblers.

Mix together the yogurt and crème fraîche. Remove the
seedy pulp from the passion fruit and set aside.

Spoon a little passion fruit pulp over the biscuits and
add about half the mango pieces.

Pour about half the crème fraîche mix over the fruit and
top with the remaining mango.

Top with the remaining crème fraîche mix and arrange
the rest of the passion fruit on top. Refrigerate for up to
1 hour or serve immediately.

For pineapple & strawberry trifle, replace the mango
with 400 g (13 oz) peeled, diced pineapple and replace
the passion fruit with 125 g (4 oz) halved strawberries.
You can also use any of the wide range of frozen fruit
available, but make sure the fruit is fully thawed first.
Continue as above. **Calories per serving 298**

chocolate sorbet

Calories per serving **295**
Serves **6–8**
Makes about **900 ml**
 (1½ pints)
Preparation time **15 minutes,**
 plus chilling and freezing
Cooking time **10 minutes**

600 ml (1 pint) **water**
150 g (5 oz) **soft dark brown
 sugar**
200 g (7 oz) **granulated
 sugar**
65 g (2½ oz) **unsweetened
 cocoa powder**
25 g (1 oz) **plain dark
 chocolate** with 70% cocoa
 solids, finely chopped
2½ teaspoons **vanilla extract**
1 teaspoon **instant espresso
 coffee powder**

Put the measured water, sugars and cocoa powder in a saucepan and mix together. Heat gently, stirring until the sugar has dissolved. Increase the heat to bring the mixture to a boil, then reduce to a simmer for 8 minutes.

Remove the pan from the heat and stir in the chocolate, vanilla extract and espresso powder until thoroughly dissolved. Pour into a bowl and cool over ice or leave to cool and chill.

Freeze in an ice-cream machine according to the manufacturer's instructions. Serve immediately or transfer to a chilled plastic freezerproof container and store in the freezer for up to 1 month. If you are using the sorbet straight from the freezer, transfer to the refrigerator 20 minutes before serving to soften slightly.

For rum & chocolate-chip sorbet, replace the vanilla extract with 3 tablespoons dark rum. Stir 75 g (3 oz) chopped plain dark chocolate into the ice-cream mixture before churning. **Calories per serving 397**

moroccan baked figs with yogurt

Calories per serving **298**
Serves **4**
Preparation time **10 minutes**
Cooking time **10 minutes**

8 **fresh figs**, rinsed in cold
water
about 3 teaspoons **rose water**
4 tablespoons **runny honey**
50 g (2 oz) **unsalted butter**
250 g (8 oz) **Greek yogurt**
a little **Turkish delight**, roughly
chopped

Cut a cross in the top of each fig and open out the cut to halfway through the fruit. Arrange the figs in a small roasting tin or shallow ovenproof dish. Add a few drops of rose water to each fig, then drizzle with 3 tablespoons of the honey and dot with the butter.

Bake in a preheated oven, 190°C (375°F), Gas Mark 5, for 8–10 minutes until the figs are hot but still firm. Meanwhile, mix the yogurt with the remaining honey and gradually mix in a little of the remaining rose water to taste.

Transfer the figs to shallow serving dishes and serve with spoonfuls of yogurt sprinkled with Turkish delight.

For orange & pistachio baked apricots, arrange 12 fresh apricots, halved, in a roasting tin. Add a few drops of orange flower water to each apricot half, then drizzle with 3 tablespoons honey and sprinkle with 40 g (1 ½ oz) halved pistachio nuts. Dot with 50 g (2 oz) butter and bake as above. Serve with 250 g (8 oz) Greek yogurt flavoured with 1 tablespoon honey and orange flower water to taste. **Calories per serving 310**

recipes under 400 calories

chai tea bread

Calories per serving **302**
Cuts into **10**
Preparation time **15 minutes**,
plus standing
Cooking time 1 ¼ **hours**

5 **chai tea bags**
300 ml (½ pint) **boiling water**
250 g (8 oz) **self-raising flour**
1 teaspoon **baking powder**
150 g (5 oz) **light muscovado
sugar**
300 g (10 oz) **mixed dried
fruit**
50 g (2 oz) **Brazil nuts**,
chopped
50 g (2 oz) **butter**
1 **egg**, beaten

Stir the tea bags into the measured water in a jug and leave to stand for 10 minutes.

Mix together the flour, baking powder, sugar, dried fruit and nuts in a bowl. Remove the tea bags from the water, pressing them against the side of the jug to squeeze out all the water. Thinly slice the butter into the water and stir until melted. Leave to cool slightly. Add to the dry ingredients with the egg and mix together well.

Spoon the mixture into a greased and lined 1 kg (2 lb) or 1.3 litre (2¼ pint) loaf tin and spread the mixture into the corners. Bake in a preheated oven, 160°C (325°F), Gas Mark 3, for 1¼ hours or until risen, firm and a skewer inserted into the centre comes out clean. Loosen the cake at the ends and transfer to a wire rack. Peel off the lining paper and leave to cool. Spread the top with chai cream frosting, if liked (see below).

For chai cream frosting, to spread over the cake, put 50 ml (2 fl oz) milk and 3 chai tea bags in a saucepan and bring to the boil. Remove from the heat and leave the tea bags to infuse in the milk until cold. Discard the tea bags, squeezing them to extract the liquid. Beat together 200 g (7 oz) cream cheese and 25 g (1 oz) very soft unsalted butter in a bowl until smooth. Beat in the flavoured milk and 75 g (3 oz) sifted icing sugar. **Calories per serving 113**

black forest brownies

Calories per serving **317**
Cuts into **12**
Preparation time **25 minutes**
Cooking time **25–30 minutes**

150 g (5 oz) **plain dark chocolate**, chopped
125 g (4 oz) **slightly salted butter**
2 **eggs**
175 g (6 oz) **dark muscovado sugar**
1 teaspoon **vanilla extract**
50 g (2 oz) **self-raising flour**
200 g (7 oz) **black** or **red cherries**, pitted and halved, plus extra to serve

To serve
150 ml (¼ pint) **double cream**
chocolate shavings

Melt 50 g (2 oz) of the chocolate and the butter in a heatproof bowl set over a saucepan of gently simmering water (don't let the base of the bowl touch the water).

Beat the eggs, sugar and vanilla in a separate bowl until light and foamy. Stir in the melted chocolate mixture. Tip in the flour, cherries and remaining chocolate and mix together until just combined.

Spoon the mixture into a greased and lined 18 cm (7 inch) square cake tin or shallow baking tin and level the surface. Bake in a preheated oven, 180°C (350°F), Gas Mark 4, for 20–25 minutes or until just firm to the touch. Leave to cool in the tin, then transfer to a board and peel off the lining paper.

Whip the cream in a bowl until peaking, then spread over the cake. Sprinkle with chocolate shavings and cut into small squares. Serve with extra cherries and rich chocolate sauce, if liked (see below).

For rich chocolate sauce, to serve as an accompaniment, heat 125 g (4 oz) caster sugar and 75 ml (3 fl oz) water in a small saucepan until the sugar dissolves. Bring to the boil and boil for 3 minutes. Remove from the heat and cool for 5 minutes. Add 150 g (5 oz) chopped plain dark chocolate and 25 g (1 oz) diced unsalted butter and leave to stand, stirring frequently, until melted and smooth. If pieces of chocolate remain, reheat the sauce very gently.
Calories per serving 128

warm chocolate fromage frais

Calories per serving **327**
Serves **6**
Preparation time **1 minute**
Cooking time **4 minutes**

300 g (10 oz) **plain dark chocolate**
500 g (1 lb) **fat-free fromage frais**
1 teaspoon **vanilla extract**

Melt the chocolate in a bowl over a pan of simmering water, then remove from the heat.

Add the fromage frais and vanilla extract and quickly stir together.

Divide the chocolate fromage frais among 6 little pots or glasses and serve immediately.

For warm cappuccino fromage frais, melt the plain dark chocolate with 2 tablespoons very strong espresso coffee and add the fat-free fromage frais. Divide among 6 espresso cups, finishing each with 1 teaspoon regular fromage frais and a dusting of cocoa powder. **Calories per serving 339**

blueberry meringue roulade

Calories per serving **336**
Cuts into **8**
Preparation time **30 minutes,**
  plus cooling
Cooking time **15 minutes**

4 **egg whites**
250 g (8 oz) **caster sugar,**
  plus extra for sprinkling
1 teaspoon **white wine**
  vinegar
1 teaspoon **cornflour**

For the filling
grated rind of 1 **lime**
300 ml (½ pint) **double**
  cream, whipped
150 g (5 oz) **blueberries**
3 **passion fruit,** halved

Whisk the egg whites in a large clean bowl until stiff. Gradually whisk in the sugar, a teaspoonful at time, until it has all been added. Whisk for a few minutes more until the meringue mixture is thick and glossy.

Combine the vinegar and cornflour then whisk into the meringue mixture. Spoon into a 33 x 23 cm (13 x 9 inch) Swiss roll tin lined with nonstick baking paper that stands a little above the top of the tin sides, then spread the surface level. Bake in a preheated oven, 190°C (375°F), Gas Mark 5, for 10 minutes until biscuit-coloured and well risen, then reduce the heat to 160°C (325°F), Gas Mark 3, for 5 minutes until just firm to the touch and the top is slightly cracked.

Meanwhile, cover a clean tea towel with nonstick baking paper and sprinkle with a little caster sugar. Turn out the meringue on to the paper. Leave to cool for 1–2 hours. Carefully peel off the lining paper.

Fold the lime rind into the whipped cream. Spread over the meringue, then sprinkle with the blueberries and passion fruit seeds. Starting with a short side and using the paper to help, roll up the meringue to form a log. Serve the same day.

For minted strawberry roulade, spread the meringue with whipped cream folded with a small bunch of mint, freshly chopped, and 250 g (8 oz) roughly chopped strawberries. Make the roulade as above and decorate with halved baby strawberries and mint leaves dusted with sifted icing sugar. **Calories per serving 335**

mango & vanilla muffin slice

Calories per serving **336**
Cuts into **8**
Preparation time **20 minutes**
Cooking time **1 hour**

1 small **ripe mango**
225 g (7½ oz) **plain flour**
2 teaspoons **baking powder**
150 g (5 oz) **golden caster sugar**
50 g (2 oz) **porridge oats**
1 **egg**, beaten
175 ml (6 fl oz) **milk**
1 teaspoon **vanilla bean paste** or extract
100 g (3½ oz) **slightly salted butter**, melted
vanilla sugar, for sprinkling

Halve the mango each side of the flat central stone. Cut away the stone, then peel and dice the flesh into 5 mm (¼ inch) pieces.

Sift the flour and baking powder into a bowl, then stir in the caster sugar and oats. Beat together the egg, milk, vanilla and melted butter in a jug. Add to the dry ingredients with half the mango and stir together using a large metal spoon until just combined.

Spoon the mixture into a greased and lined 1 kg (2 lb) or 1.3 litre (2¼ pint) loaf tin. Scatter with the remaining mango pieces and bake in a preheated oven, 180°C (350°F), Gas Mark 4, for about 1 hour or until well risen, firm to the touch and a skewer inserted into the centre comes out clean.

Leave to cool in the tin for 5 minutes, then loosen at the ends and transfer to a wire rack to cool. Peel off the lining paper and serve warm or cold, sprinkled with vanilla sugar.

For blueberry breakfast slice, put 75 g (3 oz) chopped dried blueberries and 50 ml (2 fl oz) apple or orange juice in a small saucepan and heat until the juice bubbles, then remove from the heat. Leave to cool until the juice is absorbed. Make the cake as above, omitting the mango and vanilla and adding 1 teaspoon ground cinnamon to the dry ingredients. Stir the blueberries and juice into the cake mixture. Spoon into the tin and sprinkle with 2 tablespoons porridge oats. Bake as above. **Calories per serving 385**

simple iced buns

Calories per serving **345**
Makes **10**
Preparation time **25 minutes**,
  plus proving
Cooking time **12–15 minutes**

500 g (1 lb) **strong white
  bread flour**
50 g (2 oz) **caster sugar**
1 tablespoon **fast-action
  dried yeast**
25 g (1 oz) **slightly salted
  butter**, melted
300 ml (½ pint) **hand-hot
  milk**, plus extra if required
2 teaspoons **vanilla extract**

For the icing
300 g (10 oz) **fondant icing
  sugar**
pink food colouring

Mix together the flour, sugar and yeast in a bowl. Add the butter, milk and vanilla and mix to a fairly soft dough, adding a dash more milk or hot water if the dough feels dry. Knead the dough for 10 minutes on a floured surface until smooth and elastic. Put in a lightly oiled bowl, cover with clingfilm and leave to rise in a warm place for about 1 hour or until doubled in size.

Punch the dough to deflate it, then divide into 10 even-sized pieces on a floured surface and shape each into a sausage shape. Place, well spaced apart, on a large greased baking sheet. Cover loosely with greased clingfilm and leave to rise for 30 minutes.

Bake in a preheated oven, 200°C (400°F), Gas Mark 6, for 12–15 minutes until risen and pale golden (placing a roasting tin filled with 1.5 cm (¾ inch) hot water on the lower shelf to prevent a firm crust forming). Transfer to a wire rack to cool.

Make the icing. Sift the icing sugar into a bowl and gradually beat in a little water, a teaspoonful at a time, to make a smooth, spreadable icing. Spread half over 5 of the buns. Add a dash of pink food colouring to the remaining icing and spread over the rest of the buns. Best eaten freshly baked.

For sticky currant buns, make the dough as above, adding ½ teaspoon ground cinnamon and 175 g (6 oz) mixed dried fruit. Leave to prove as above. Shape into 10 balls and flatten slightly on the baking sheet. Brush with a little milk and bake as above. Heat 2 tablespoons golden syrup in a saucepan and brush over the cooled buns. **Calories per serving 286**

passion fruit yogurt fool

Calories per serving **347**

Serves **4**

Preparation time **8 minutes**

6 **passion fruit**, halved, flesh
and seeds removed

300 ml (½ pint) **fat-free Greek
yogurt**

1 tablespoon **clear honey**

200 ml (7 fl oz) **whipping
cream**, whipped to soft
peaks

4 pieces of **shortbread**, to
serve

Stir the passion fruit flesh and seeds into the yogurt
with the honey.

Fold the cream into the yogurt. Spoon into tall glasses
and serve with the shortbread.

For mango & lime yogurt fool, omit the passion fruit,
instead puréeing 1 large ripe peeled and stoned mango
with the zest of 1 lime and icing sugar to taste. Mix
into the yogurt and fold in the cream. Omit the honey.
Calories per serving 358

spiced bananas

Calories per serving **348**
Serves **8**
Preparation time **10 minutes**
Cooking time **10 minutes**

8 **bananas**, peeled
2 tablespoons **lemon juice**
8 tablespoons **light muscovado sugar**
50 g (2 oz) **butter**, softened
1 teaspoon **cinnamon**

Rum mascarpone cream
250 g (8 oz) **mascarpone cheese**
2 tablespoons **rum**
1–2 tablespoons **granulated sugar**

Put each banana on a double piece of foil. Drizzle over the lemon juice and sprinkle 1 tablespoon of the muscovado sugar on each banana.

Beat together the butter and cinnamon in a bowl until creamy, then spoon over the bananas. Wrap each banana tightly in the foil and cook over a barbecue or under a preheated medium grill for 10 minutes.

Meanwhile, make the rum mascarpone cream. Mix together the mascarpone, rum and sugar in a bowl.

Unwrap the bananas and slice thickly. Serve immediately with the rum mascarpone cream.

For BBQ pineapple with rum butter glaze, cut off the top and base of 1 large fresh pineapple and slice off the skin, then cut into quarters and remove the core from each quarter. Slice the quarters across into 2.5 cm (1 inch) thick triangular slices. Sprinkle both sides with a little caster sugar and cook over a barbecue for 5–6 minutes or until lightly caramelized. Meanwhile, melt 75g (3 oz) butter in a small pan, then add 75g (3 oz) demerara sugar and the juice of ½ lime. Scrape out the seeds of 1 vanilla pod and add to the pan with 2 tablespoons dark rum. Stir until the mixture has melted and bubbled to form a smooth glaze. Place the pineapple slices on a plate, spoon over the rum butter and serve immediately with 1 scoop ice cream per slice. **Calories per serving 248**

pears with minted mascarpone

Calories per serving **358**
Serves **4**
Preparation time **10 minutes**
Cooking time **5 minutes**

30 g (1 ¼ oz) **unsalted butter**
2 tablespoons **clear honey**
4 ripe **dessert pears**, such
   as Red William, cored and
   quartered lengthways
lemon juice, for sprinkling

Minted mascarpone
1 tablespoon **fresh mint**,
   finely chopped
1 tablespoon **granulated
   sugar**
175 g (6 oz) **mascarpone
   cheese**

To decorate
fresh mint sprigs
icing sugar, sifted
ground cinnamon

Melt the butter in a small saucepan. Remove the pan from the heat and stir in the honey.

Sprinkle the pear slices with a little lemon juice as soon as they are cut to prevent them from discolouring. Line a baking sheet with foil and lay the pear slices on it. Brush the pears with the butter and honey mixture and cook under a preheated grill on its highest setting for 5 minutes.

Meanwhile, make the minted mascarpone. Lightly whisk the mint and granulated sugar into the mascarpone in a bowl.

Arrange the pear slices on 4 plates and top each with a spoonful of the minted mascarpone. Decorate with mint sprigs, then lightly dust with icing sugar and cinnamon and serve immediately.

For pear & jam tarts, lay out 200 g (7 oz) ready-rolled puff pastry, thawed if frozen, on a floured surface and cut out 4 circles using an 18 cm (7 inch) plate as a template. Transfer the circles to 2 greased baking sheets. Peel, core and finely slice the pears and place in a bowl. Toss with just enough caster sugar to coat the fruit and 2 tablespoons freshly squeezed orange juice. Place 1 tablespoon any flavoured jam in the middle of each pastry circle, fan out the fruit slices on top and fold in the sides of the pastry to hold it all together. Bake in a preheated oven, 220°C (425°F), Gas Mark 7, for 10–12 minutes until the fruit has softened and the pastry is crisp and golden. Serve with 1 scoop vanilla ice cream per tart. **Calories per serving 401**

watermelon & choc-chip sorbet

Calories per serving **358**
Serves **8**
Preparation time **20 minutes**,
  plus chilling and freezing
Cooking time **5 minutes**

750 g (1½ lb) **peeled
  watermelon**, deseeded and
  cubed
300 g (10 oz) **caster sugar**
8 tablespoons **lemon juice**
pink food colouring (optional)
1 **egg white**
125 g (4 oz) **chocolate chips**

Purée the watermelon in a food processor or blender. Add the sugar and process for 30 seconds.

Pour into a saucepan and bring slowly to the boil, stirring until the sugar has dissolved, then simmer for 1 minute. Remove from the heat, add the lemon juice, then leave to cool, adding a few drops of pink food colouring, if liked. Chill for at least 1 hour or overnight.

Use an ice-cream machine for the best results. Half-freeze the mixture according to the manufacturer's instructions, then lightly whisk the egg white and add with the motor still running. Stir in the chocolate chips, then transfer to a plastic freezerproof container and freeze until firm.

Alternatively, freeze the mixture in a shallow freezer tray until frozen around the edges, then mash well with a fork. Whisk the egg white until stiff in a bowl. Drop spoonfuls of the sorbet into the egg white while whisking constantly with a hand-held electric whisk until the mixture is thick and foamy. Return to the freezer to firm up, then stir in the chocolate chips when almost frozen. Freeze until firm.

Transfer the sorbet to the refrigerator for 20 minutes before serving to soften. Serve with dessert biscuits.

For watermelon & orange sorbet, omit the chocolate chips. Reduce the quantity of watermelon to 500 g (1 lb) and process to a purée. Heat the sugar in a pan with 250 ml (8 fl oz) freshly squeezed orange juice, stirring until dissolved. Once cooled combine the watermelon, sweetened orange juice and lemon juice. Freeze as above. **Calories per serving 246**

mixed berry chocolate roulade

Calories per serving **364**
Serves **4**
Preparation time **20 minutes**,
   plus cooling
Cooking time **15 minutes**

3 **large eggs**
100 g (3½ oz) **caster sugar**
½ teaspoon **chocolate extract**
50 g (2 oz) **plain flour**
25 g (1 oz) **cocoa**, plus extra
   to dust
150 g (5 oz) **half-fat crème
   fraîche**
150 g (5 oz) **fat-free Greek
   yogurt**
25 g (1 oz) **icing sugar**
1 tablespoon **chocolate
   sauce**
200 g (7 oz) **mixed berries**,
   chopped, plus extra to
   decorate

Grease and line a 30 x 20 cm (12 x 8 inch) Swiss roll tin. Whisk together the eggs and sugar until the mixer leaves a trail over the surface. Add the chocolate extract, sift in the flour and cocoa and fold in carefully.

Pour the mixture into the prepared tin. Bake in a preheated oven, 200°C (400°F), Gas Mark 6, for 15 minutes. Place a clean tea towel on the work surface and put a piece of nonstick baking paper on top. When the sponge is cooked, turn it out on to the baking paper, roll it up carefully and leave to cool.

Mix together the crème fraîche, yogurt, icing sugar and chocolate sauce.

Unroll the roulade and spread the crème fraîche mix over it. Spoon the berries over the crème fraîche and roll up the roulade again. Dust with cocoa and serve immediately, decorated with extra berries.

For strawberry & vanilla roulade, omit the cocoa, increase the plain flour to 75 g (3 oz) and use ½ teaspoon vanilla extract instead of the chocolate extract. Use 200 g (7 oz) strawberries to fill the roulade and serve decorated with extra sliced strawberries, if liked. **Calories per serving 381**

peach & blueberry crunch

Calories per serving **371**
Serves **4**
Preparation time **8 minutes**
Cooking time **8–10 minutes**

25 g (1 oz) **ground hazelnuts**
25 g (1 oz) **ground almonds**
25 g (1 oz) **caster sugar**
25 g (1 oz) **breadcrumbs**
410 g (13½ oz) can **peaches**
  in natural juice
125 g (4 oz) **blueberries**
150 ml (¼ pint) **double cream**
seeds from 1 **vanilla pod**
1 tablespoon **icing sugar,**
  sifted

Gently cook the ground nuts in a large frying pan with the sugar and breadcrumbs, stirring constantly until golden. Remove from the heat and leave to cool.

Put the peaches in a food processor or blender and blend with enough of the peach juice to make a thick, smooth purée.

Set aside some of the blueberries to decorate and fold the remaining blueberries gently into the purée. Spoon into 4 glasses or individual serving dishes.

Whip the cream with the vanilla seeds and icing sugar until thick but not stiff and spoon evenly over the peach purée. When the crunchy topping is cool, sprinkle it over the blueberry mixture, top with the remaining blueberries and serve.

For apple & blackberry biscuit crunch, peel 450 g (14½ oz) cooking apples and cook with 2–3 tablespoons sugar and 2 tablespoons water. Fold 125 g (4 oz) blackberries into the apple purée and continue as above, but instead of breadcrumbs, use crushed digestive biscuits. Use the same amount and toast in the same way, but reduce the sugar to 1 tablespoon. **Calories per serving 393**

date & banana ripple slice

Calories per serving **373**

Cuts into **10**

Preparation time **20 minutes**,
plus cooling

Cooking time **1 hour 25
minutes**

250 g (8 oz) **stoned dates**,
roughly chopped

finely grated rind and juice of
1 lemon

100 ml (3½ fl oz) **water**

2 small very **ripe bananas**

150 g (5 oz) **slightly salted
butter**, softened

150 g (5 oz) **caster sugar**

2 **eggs**

100 ml (3½ fl oz) **milk**

275 g (9 oz) **self-raising flour**

1 teaspoon **baking powder**

Put 200 g (7 oz) of the dates in a small saucepan with
the lemon rind and juice and measured water. Bring to
the boil, then reduce the heat and simmer gently for
5 minutes until the dates are soft and pulpy. Mash the
mixture with a fork until fairly smooth. Leave to cool.

Mash the bananas to a purée in a bowl, then add the
butter, sugar, eggs, milk, flour and baking powder and
beat together until smooth.

Spoon a third of the mixture into a greased and lined
1.25 kg (2½ lb) or 1.5 litre (2½ pint) loaf tin and level
the surface. Spoon over half the date purée and spread
evenly. Add half the remaining cake mixture and spread
with the remaining purée. Add the remaining cake
mixture and level the surface.

Scatter with the remaining dates and bake in a
preheated oven, 160°C (325°F), Gas Mark 3, for about
1 hour 20 minutes or until risen and a skewer inserted
into the centre comes out clean. Leave to cool in the tin
for 15 minutes, then loosen at the ends and transfer to
a wire rack. Peel off the lining paper and leave the cake
to cool completely.

For honeyed banana cake, make the cake as above,
omitting all the dates. For the honey buttercream,
beat together 150 g (5 oz) softened unsalted butter,
6 tablespoons sifted icing sugar and 6 tablespoons
clear honey in a bowl until smooth and creamy.
Spread over the top of the cooled cake. **Calories
per serving 447**

chocolate cupcakes

Calories per serving **374**
Makes **12**
Preparation time **10 minutes**,
  plus cooling
Cooking time **18–20 minutes**
Decoration time **20 minutes**

150 g (5 oz) **butter** or
  margarine
150 g (5 oz) **caster sugar**
175 g (6 oz) **self-raising flour**
3 **eggs**
1 teaspoon **vanilla extract**

To decorate
100 g (3½ oz) **white**
  chocolate, chopped
100 g (3½ oz) **milk**
  chocolate, chopped
100 g (3½ oz) **plain dark**
  chocolate, chopped
40 g (1½ oz) **butter**
cocoa powder, for dusting

Whisk the butter or margarine, sugar, flour, eggs and vanilla extract in a mixing bowl until light and creamy.

Line a 12-hole muffin tray with paper cases. Divide the mixture evenly among the cases and bake in a preheated oven, 180°C (350°F), Gas Mark 4, for 18–20 minutes until risen and just firm to the touch. Transfer to a wire rack to cool.

Melt the white, milk and plain dark chocolate in 3 separate bowls, each with one-third of the butter added, over pans of simmering water. Spread the melted white chocolate over 4 of the cakes and dust with a little cocoa powder.

Put 2 tablespoons each of the melted milk chocolate and plain dark chocolate in separate piping bags fitted with writing nozzles. Spread the milk chocolate over 4 more of the cakes and pipe dots of plain dark chocolate over the milk chocolate. Spread the plain dark chocolate over the 4 remaining cakes and scribble with lines of piped milk chocolate.

For triple chocolate cupcakes, substitute 15 g (½ oz) cocoa powder for 15 g (½ oz) of the self-raising flour and add 50 g (2 oz) chopped white chocolate. Prepare the mixture and bake as above. Decorate the cooled cakes with white chocolate fudge icing made by melting 250 g (8 oz) white chocolate with 125 ml (4 fl oz) single cream and 75 g (3 oz) butter. Cool, then beat until thick and fluffy before piping a large swirl on each cake.
Calories per serving 412

ricotta & maple syrup cheesecake

Calories per serving **375**
Serves **8**
Preparation time **20 minutes**,
   plus chilling

3 **gelatine leaves**
125 g (4 oz) **digestive
   biscuits**, crushed
50 g (2 oz) **reduced-fat
   sunflower spread**, melted
200 g (7 oz) **cottage cheese**
200 g (7 oz) **ricotta cheese**
2 **egg whites**
25 g (1 oz) **icing sugar**, sieved
25 ml (1 fl oz) **lemon juice**
4 tablespoons **maple syrup**

To decorate
2 **oranges**, peeled and sliced
sprigs of **redcurrants**

Line a 20 cm (8 inch) springform tin with nonstick
baking paper. Soften the gelatine in cold water.

Mix together the biscuit crumbs and melted sunflower
spread and press into the prepared tin. Refrigerate.

Sieve together the cottage cheese and ricotta. Beat the
egg whites until stiffly peaking, then beat in the icing
sugar until glossy.

Put the lemon juice and 50 ml (2 fl oz) water in a
saucepan over a low heat and stir in the gelatine until
dissolved. Add to the ricotta mix with the maple syrup,
then fold in the egg whites. Pour the mixture over the
biscuit base and refrigerate until set.

Decorate with the sliced oranges and sprigs of
redcurrants before serving.

**For raspberry & ricotta cheesecake with chocolate
sauce**, stir 250 g (8 oz) raspberries into the pan with
the ricotta mix, then make the cheesecake as above.
To serve, melt 100 g (3½ oz) plain chocolate with
4 tablespoons syrup and drizzle over the cheesecake.
Calories per serving 460

192

instant apple crumbles

Calories per serving **379**
Serves **4**
Preparation time **7 minutes**
Cooking time **13 minutes**

1 kg (2 lb) **Bramley apples**,
  peeled, cored and thickly
  sliced
25 g (1 oz) **butter**
2 tablespoons **caster sugar**
1 tablespoon **lemon juice**
2 tablespoons **water**

Crumble
50 g (2 oz) **butter**
75 g (3 oz) fresh **wholemeal
  breadcrumbs**
25 g (1 oz) **pumpkin seeds**
2 tablespoons **soft brown
  sugar**

Place the apples in a saucepan with the butter, sugar, lemon juice and measured water. Cover and simmer for 8–10 minutes, until softened.

Melt the butter for the crumble in a frying pan, add the breadcrumbs and stir-fry until lightly golden, then add the pumpkin seeds and stir-fry for a further 1 minute. Remove from the heat and stir in the brown sugar.

Spoon the apple mixture into bowls and sprinkle with the crumble.

For instant pear & chocolate crumble, cook 1 kg (2 lb) pears in the butter, sugar and water as above, adding ½ teaspoon ground ginger to the butter. Prepare the crumble as above, replacing the pumpkin seeds with 50 g (2 oz) roughly chopped plain chocolate. Cook as above. **Calories per serving 424**

poached fruit with ginger biscuits

Calories per serving **391**

Serves **6**

Preparation time **15 minutes**

Cooking time **20 minutes**

250 g (8 oz) **caster sugar**

2.5 litres (4 pints) **water**

1 **vanilla pod**, plus extra for decorating if liked

4 **peaches**

4 **nectarines**

10 **apricots**

To serve

mascarpone cheese

3 **ginger biscuits**, crushed

Put the sugar, measured water and vanilla pod in a large, heavy-based saucepan and heat gently, stirring, until the sugar has dissolved. Bring to a low simmer, add the fruit and cover with a circle of greaseproof or baking parchment to hold the fruit in the syrup. Simmer for 2 minutes, then turn off the heat and leave to cool.

Remove the fruit from the liquid with a slotted spoon, reserving the poaching liquid. Peel the skins from the fruit, then cut them in half and remove the stones.

Put 250 ml (8 fl oz) of the poaching liquid in a small, heavy-based saucepan and heat to reduce it for 6–8 minutes until it has a syrupy consistency. Put the fruit in a large bowl, pour over the syrup and toss gently. Arrange the fruit on serving plates, add 1 rounded tablespoon mascarpone to each one and sprinkle with crushed ginger biscuits. Decorate with a vanilla pod, if liked.

For poached stone fruit with raspberry coulis, put 150 g (5 oz) frozen raspberries and 40 g (1½ oz) caster sugar in a heavy-based saucepan. Slowly bring up to the boil, stirring, to dissolve the sugar. Simmer for 2–3 minutes until the coulis has a syrupy consistency. Remove from the heat and strain through a fine sieve. Poach the stone fruit as above and serve with the raspberry coulis and a drizzle of custard. **Calories per serving 322**

granola squares

Calories per serving **399**
Makes **12**
Preparation time **15 minutes**,
 plus chilling
Cooking time **20 minutes**

175 g (6 oz) **butter**, plus extra
 for greasing
150 ml (¼ pint) **clear honey**
2 tablespoons **maple syrup**
1 teaspoon **ground cinnamon**
125 g (4 oz) ready-to-eat
 dried apricots, roughly
 chopped
100 g (4 oz) ready-to-eat
 dried papaya or **mango**,
 roughly chopped
125 g (4 oz) **raisins**
4 tablespoons **pumpkin
 seeds**
2 tablespoons **sesame seeds**
3 tablespoons **sunflower
 seeds**
75 g (3 oz) **pecan nuts**,
 roughly chopped
275 g (9 oz) **porridge oats**

Grease a 28 x 18 cm (11 x 7 inch) deep Swiss roll tin with butter and line the base with nonstick baking paper.

Place the butter, honey and maple syrup in a medium saucepan and heat, stirring continually, until the butter has melted. Add the cinnamon, dried fruit, seeds and nuts, stir the mixture and heat for 1 minute. Remove from the heat and add the porridge oats, stirring until they are well coated in the syrup.

Transfer the mixture to the prepared tin and smooth down with the back of a spoon to compact into the tin and level. Bake in a preheated oven, 180°C (350°F), Gas Mark 4, for 15 minutes until the top is just beginning to brown. Remove from the oven and allow to cool in the tin, then chill in the refrigerator for 30–60 minutes.

Turn out the chilled granola, upside down, on a chopping board, then carefully flip it back over to its correct side. Using a long, sharp knife (preferably longer than the granola itself), cut into 12 squares.

For fruity chocolate granola squares, leave out the pecans and seeds and replace with 75 g (3 oz) roughly chopped ready-to-eat dried apples. Once cooled, drizzle 50 g (2 oz) melted white chocolate over the top. Allow to set in the refrigerator for 10 minutes before cutting into squares. **Calories per serving 360**

recipes
under 500
calories

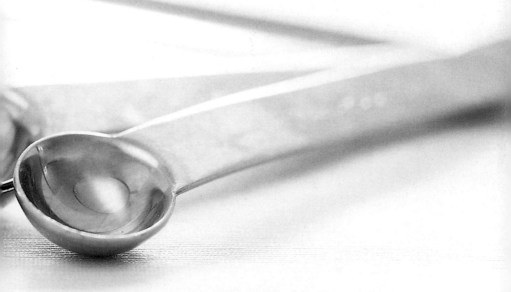

lemon drizzle cake

Calories per serving **400**
Cuts into **8**
Preparation time **20 minutes**
Cooking time **22–28 minutes**

5 **eggs**
100 g (3½ oz) **caster sugar**
pinch of **salt**
125 g (4 oz) **plain flour**
1 teaspoon **baking powder**
finely grated rind of 1 **lemon**
1 tablespoon **lemon juice**
100 g (3½ oz) **butter**, melted
and cooled

For the syrup
250 g (8 oz) **icing sugar**,
sifted
125 ml (4 fl oz) **lemon juice**
finely grated rind of 1 **lemon**
seeds scraped from 1 **vanilla
pod**

Put the eggs, sugar and salt in a large heatproof bowl set over a saucepan of barely simmering water and beat with a hand-held electric whisk for 2–3 minutes or until it triples in volume and thickens to the consistency of lightly whipped cream. Remove from the heat. Sift in the flour and baking powder, add the lemon rind and juice and drizzle the butter down the side of the bowl. Fold in gently.

Pour the mixture into a greased and lined 22 cm (8½ inch) square cake tin. Bake in a preheated oven, 180°C (350°F), Gas Mark 4, for 20–25 minutes or until risen, golden and coming away from the sides of the tin.

Meanwhile, put all the syrup ingredients in a small saucepan and heat gently until the sugar dissolves. Increase the heat and boil rapidly for 4–5 minutes. Set aside to cool a little.

Leave the cake to cool in the tin for 5 minutes, then make holes over the surface with a skewer. Drizzle over two-thirds of the warm syrup. Leave the cake to cool and absorb the syrup. Turn the cake out of the tin and peel off the lining paper. Cut into squares or slices and serve with 1 heaped teaspoon of half-fat crème fraîche or soured cream and an extra drizzle of syrup.

For citrus drizzle cake with sorbet, make the cake as above, replacing the lemon rind and juice with the finely grated rind of 1 orange and 1 tablespoon orange juice. Serve topped with lemon sorbet. **Calories per serving 391**

tuile baskets & strawberry cream

Calories per serving **404**
Serves **6**
Preparation time **40 minutes**
Cooking time **15–18 minutes**

2 **egg whites**
100 g (3½ oz) **caster sugar**
50 g (2 oz) **unsalted butter**,
  melted
few drops **vanilla essence**
50 g (2 oz) **plain flour**

Strawberry cream
250 ml (8 fl oz) **double cream**
4 tablespoons **icing sugar**,
  plus extra for dusting
2 tablespoons **chopped fresh
  mint**, plus extra leaves to
  decorate
250 g (8 oz) **strawberries**,
  halved or sliced, depending
  on size

Put the egg whites in a bowl and break up with a fork.
Stir in the caster sugar, then the butter and vanilla
essence. Sift in the flour and mix until smooth.

Drop 1 heaped tablespoon of the mixture on to a
baking sheet lined with nonstick baking paper. Drop a
second spoonful well apart from the first, then spread
each into a thin circle about 13 cm (5 inches) in
diameter. Bake in a preheated oven, 190°C (375°F),
Gas Mark 5, for 5–6 minutes until just beginning to
brown around the edges.

Add 2 more spoonfuls to a second paper-lined baking
sheet and spread thinly. Remove the baked tuiles from
the oven and put the second tray in. Allow the cooked
tuiles to firm up for 5–10 seconds, then carefully lift
them off the paper one at a time and drape each over
an orange. Pinch the edges into pleats and leave to
harden for 2–3 minutes, then carefully ease off.
Repeat until 6 tuiles have been made.

Whip the cream lightly, then fold in half the sugar, the
mint and the strawberries, reserving 6 strawberry halves
for decoration. Spoon into the tuiles, then top with the
mint leaves and the strawberry halves. Dust with sifted
icing sugar.

For fruit salad baskets, make the tuiles as above and
fill with 200 g (7 oz) sliced strawberries, 150 g (5 oz)
halved seedless ruby grapes, 2 kiwifruits, peeled, halved
and sliced, and 2 small ripe peaches. Top each one
with 1 tablespoon Greek yogurt and 1 teaspoon honey.
Calories per serving 247

caramelized clementines with bay

Calories per serving **405**
Serves **4**
Preparation time **10 minutes**
Cooking time **12 minutes**

250 g (8 oz) **granulated sugar**
250 ml (8 fl oz) **cold water**
8 **clementines**
4 small **fresh bay leaves**
6 tablespoons **boiling water**
4 tablespoons **crème fraîche**, to serve

Put the sugar and measured cold water in a saucepan and heat gently, stirring very occasionally until the sugar has completely dissolved.

Meanwhile, peel the clementines and, leaving them whole, place in a heavy glass serving bowl or mixing bowl with the bay leaves.

Increase the heat once the sugar has dissolved and boil the syrup for 8–10 minutes, without stirring and keeping a close watch on it until it begins to change colour, first becoming pale golden around the edges, then a rich golden colour all over.

Take the pan off the heat, then add the measured boiling water, a tablespoon at a time, standing well back in case the syrup spits. Tilt the pan to mix but don't stir. Once the bubbles have subsided, pour the hot syrup over the clementines and bay leaves. Leave to cool, then serve the dessert with 1 tablespoon crème fraîche per person.

For caramelized clementines with whole spices, omit the bay leaves and add 2 whole star anise or the equivalent in pieces, 1 cinnamon stick, halved, and 3 cloves to the clementines. Make the syrup as above, then pour it over the spices and fruit. **Calories per serving 405**

layered nutty bars

Calories per serving **406**
Cuts into **10**
Preparation time **20 minutes**,
  plus chilling
Cooking time **5 minutes**

50 g (2 oz) **butter**
400 g (13 oz) **fat-free
  sweetened condensed
  milk**
200 g (7 oz) **plain dark
  chocolate**, broken into
  pieces
125 g (4 oz) **rich tea biscuits**
50 g (2 oz) **hazelnuts**
100 g (3½ oz) **pistachio nuts**,
  shelled

Use a little of the butter to grease the base and sides of a 20 cm (8 inch) round spring-form tin. Put the rest of the butter in a saucepan with the condensed milk and chocolate. Heat gently for 3–4 minutes, stirring until melted, then remove from the heat.

Place the biscuits in a plastic bag and crush roughly into chunky pieces using a rolling pin. Toast the hazelnuts under a preheated hot grill until lightly browned, then roughly chop with the pistachios.

Stir the biscuits into the chocolate mixture, then spoon half the mixture into the prepared tin and spread level. Reserve 2 tablespoons of the nuts for the top, then sprinkle the rest over the chocolate biscuit layer. Cover with the remaining chocolate mixture, level the surface with the back of the spoon and sprinkle with the reserved nuts.

Chill the nut mixture for 3–4 hours until firm, then loosen the edges and remove the sides of the tin. Cut into 10 thin slices, or into tiny bite-sized pieces to make petits fours. Store any leftovers in the refrigerator, wrapped in foil, for up to 3 days.

For gingered fruit bars, make the chocolate mix as above and stir in crushed digestive biscuits instead of the rich tea biscuits. Omit the nuts and use 50 g (2 oz) roughly chopped ready-to-eat dried apricots and 2 tablespoons chopped glacé ginger, keeping 2–3 tablespoons back for the topping. **Calories per serving 351**

hot caribbean fruit salad

Calories per serving **408**
Serves **4**
Preparation time **15 minutes**
Cooking time **6–7 minutes**

50 g (2 oz) **unsalted butter**
50 g (2 oz) **light muscovado
  sugar**
1 **large papaya**, halved,
  deseeded, peeled and sliced
1 **large mango**, pitted, peeled
  and sliced
½ **pineapple**, cored, peeled
  and cut into chunks
400 ml (14 fl oz) can **full-fat
  coconut milk**
grated rind and juice of 1 **lime**

Heat the butter in a large frying pan, add the sugar and heat gently until just dissolved. Add all the fruit and cook for 2 minutes, then pour in the coconut milk, half the lime rind and all the juice.

Heat gently for 4–5 minutes, then serve warm in shallow bowls, sprinkled with the remaining lime rind.

For flamed Caribbean fruit salad, omit the coconut milk and add 3 tablespoons dark or white rum. When the rum is bubbling, flame with a long match and stand well back. When the flames have subsided, add the lime rind and juice and serve. **Calories per serving 252**

pistachio & yogurt semifreddo

Calories per serving **416**
Serves **6**
Preparation time **40 minutes**,
   plus cooling and freezing
Cooking time **10–15 minutes**

4 **eggs**, separated
175 g (6 oz) **caster sugar**
grated rind of 1 **lemon**
1½ teaspoons **rose water**
   (optional)
200 g (7 oz) **Greek yogurt**
½ **fresh pineapple**, sliced,
   halved and cored

Pistachio brittle
150 g (5 oz) **granulated**
   sugar
6 tablespoons **water**
100 g (3½ oz) **pistachio nuts**,
   roughly chopped

Make the brittle. Heat the sugar and measured water in a frying pan until it dissolves, stirring gently from time to time. Add the nuts, then increase the heat and boil the syrup for 5 minutes, without stirring, until pale golden. Quickly tip the mixture on to a greased baking sheet and leave to cool. Break the brittle in half, then crush half in a plastic bag with a rolling pin.

Whisk the egg whites until very stiff, then gradually whisk in half the sugar until thick and glossy. Whisk the egg yolks in a second bowl with the remaining sugar until very thick and pale and the mixture leaves a trail. Fold in the lemon rind and rose water, if using, then the yogurt and crushed brittle, then the egg whites. Pour into a plastic box and freeze for 4–5 hours until semi-frozen and firm enough to scoop.

Cook the pineapple slices on a hot barbecue or preheated griddle pan for 6–8 minutes, turning once or twice until browned. Divide between the serving plates, top with spoonfuls of semifreddo and decorate with broken pieces of the remaining brittle.

For rocky road ice cream, make the brittle with almonds, hazelnuts and pecan nuts instead of pistachios. Whisk the egg whites, then the eggs and sugar, as for the semifreddo, then fold 135 g (4½ oz) ready-made custard and 150 ml (¼ pint) whipped double cream into the yolks with the crushed brittle. Fold in the egg whites as above, then freeze. Serve scooped into glasses. **Calories per serving 410**

summer berry sponge

Calories per serving **422**
Serves **6**
Preparation time **30 minutes**,
 plus cooling
Cooking time **10–12 minutes**

4 **eggs**
100 g (3½ oz) **caster sugar**
100 g (3½ oz) **plain flour**
finely grated rind and
 2 tablespoons juice of
 1 **lemon**
150 ml (¼ pint) **double cream**
150 g (5 oz) **fromage frais**
3 tablespoons **lemon curd**
500 g (1 lb) small
 strawberries, halved
150 g (5 oz) **blueberries**
4 tablespoons **redcurrant jelly**
1 tablespoon water (or **lemon
 juice**)

Whisk the eggs and caster sugar in a large bowl until very thick and the mixture leaves a trail when lifted. Sift the flour over the surface of the eggs, then fold in very gently. Add the lemon rind and juice and fold in until just mixed. Pour the mixture into a greased, floured 25 cm (10 inch) sponge flan tin, tilting the tin to ease into an even layer.

Bake in a preheated oven, 180°C (350°F), Gas Mark 4, for 10–12 minutes until the top of the sponge is golden and the centre springs back when lightly pressed. Cool the sponge in the tin for 5–10 minutes, then carefully turn it out on to a wire rack to cool.

Whip the cream until it forms soft swirls, then fold in the fromage frais and lemon curd. Transfer the sponge to a serving plate, spoon the cream into the centre, spread into an even layer, then top with the strawberries and blueberries. Warm the redcurrant jelly in a small saucepan with the measured water (or lemon juice), then brush over the fruit.

For strawberry sponge flan with Pimm's, make the sponge flan as above, then fill with 300 ml (½ pint) whipped cream flavoured with the grated rind of ½ orange. Top with 500 g (1 lb) sliced strawberries and 150 g (5 oz) raspberries that have been soaked in 3 tablespoons undiluted Pimm's and 2 tablespoons caster sugar for 30 minutes. **Calories per serving 491**

toffee peaches

Calories per serving **424**
Serves **4**
Preparation time **10 minutes**
Cooking time **15 minutes**

4 **peaches**, halved and stoned
50 g (2 oz) **ground almonds**

Sauce
125 (4 oz) **soft light brown
  sugar**
5 tablespoons **maple syrup**
25 g (1 oz) **butter**
150 ml (¼ pint) **single cream**

Cut 4 x 20 cm (8 inch) square pieces of foil and place 2 peach halves in each. Sprinkle over the ground almonds. Scrunch up the foil to form 4 parcels and place under a preheated medium grill for 5–8 minutes, turning once or twice during cooking until the peaches are soft.

Meanwhile, make the sauce. Place the sugar, maple syrup and butter in a nonstick saucepan over a moderately low heat until the sugar dissolves. Stir continuously until the sauce boils and thickens, which should take about 3 minutes. Add the cream and return to the boil, then immediately remove from the heat.

Drizzle the sauce over the peaches, and serve.

For toffee apples, place 4 halved apples in sheets of foil and divide 15 g (½ oz) butter between them in cubes, dotting over the top. Sprinkle with a little ground cinnamon and grill for 10–12 minutes until the apples have softened, yet still retain their shape. Serve with the sauce as above. **Calories per serving 383**

216

pears with maple syrup biscuits

Calories per serving **431**

Serves **4**

Preparation time **20 minutes**

Cooking time **50 minutes**

2 **vanilla pods**, split

3 tablespoons **clear honey**

375 ml (13 fl oz) **sweet white wine**

125 g (4 oz) **caster sugar**

200 ml (7 fl oz) **water**

4 **hard pears**, such as Packham or Comice, peeled, cored and halved

Maple syrup biscuits

25 g (1 oz) **reduced-fat sunflower spread**

2 tablespoons **maple syrup**

1 tablespoon **caster sugar**

50 g (2 oz) **plain flour**

1 **egg white**

Combine the vanilla pods, honey, wine, sugar and water in a saucepan large enough to hold all the pears. Heat until the sugar dissolves and then add the pears. Simmer for 30 minutes or until the pears are very tender. Remove the pears from the pan with a slotted spoon and set aside.

Simmer the syrup for about 15 minutes until it has reduced. Set aside with the pears until ready to serve.

Make the biscuits. Beat together the sunflower spread, maple syrup and sugar, then stir in the flour. Beat the egg white until softly peaking, then fold it into the mix.

Drop teaspoonfuls of the mixture on to a lightly greased baking sheet, spacing the biscuits well apart. Bake in a preheated oven, 200°C (400°F), Gas Mark 6, for about 8 minutes until golden. Remove and transfer to a rack to cool.

Decorate the pears with a sliver of vanilla pod and serve with a little syrup drizzled over them and a biscuit on the side.

For vanilla & rose water peaches, replace the pears with the same quantity of peaches and poach in the syrup as above for about 20 minutes or until tender. Halved peaches will take less time. Remove the peaches and continue to simmer the syrup for about 15 minutes until it has reduced. Add 1–2 tablespoons rose water, to taste, for a more fragrant syrup. Finish as above. **Calories per serving 420**

toffee & banana pancakes

Calories per serving **438**
Serves **6**
Preparation time **15 minutes**,
   plus resting
Cooking time **30 minutes**

100 g (3½ oz) **plain flour**
pinch **salt**
1 **egg**
1 **egg yolk**
300 ml (½ pint) **milk**
2–3 tablespoons **sunflower
   oil**
2 **bananas**, sliced

Toffee sauce
50 g (2 oz) **unsalted butter**
50 g (2 oz) **light muscovado
   sugar**
2 tablespoons **golden syrup**
150 ml (¼ pint) **double cream**

Sift the flour into a bowl, add the salt, egg and egg yolk, then gradually whisk in the milk to make a smooth batter. Set aside for 30 minutes.

Put the butter, sugar and syrup for the toffee sauce in a small saucepan and heat gently, stirring occasionally, until the butter has melted and the sugar dissolved. Bring to the boil and cook for 3–4 minutes until just beginning to darken around the edges.

Take the pan off the heat, then gradually pour in the cream. Tilt the pan to mix and as the bubbles subside stir with a wooden spoon. Set aside.

Pour the oil for cooking the pancakes into an 18 cm (7 inch) frying pan, heat and then pour off the excess into a small bowl or jug. Pour a little pancake batter over the base of the pan, tilt the pan to coat the base evenly with batter, then cook for 2 minutes until the underside is golden. Loosen with a palette knife, turn over and cook the second side in the same way. When cooked, slide on to a plate and keep hot. Cook the remaining batter, oiling the pan as needed.

Fold the pancakes and arrange on serving plates. Top with banana slices and drizzle with the toffee sauce.

For citrus pancakes, make the pancakes as above, then drizzle them with the freshly squeezed juice of 1 lemon and 1 orange. Sprinkle with 50 g (2 oz) caster sugar before serving. **Calories per serving 200**

cherries with cinnamon crumble

Calories per serving **440**
Serves **4–6**
Preparation time **15 minutes**,
  plus cooling
Cooking time **20 minutes**

1.5 kg (3 lb) **cherries**, pitted
250 g (8 oz) **caster sugar**
400 ml (14 fl oz) **water**
1 **vanilla pod**
2 **cloves**
strips of **orange peel**, to
  decorate

Crumble
60 g (2¼ oz) **fruit loaf**
15 g (¼ oz) **unsalted butter**
⅛ teaspoon **ground
  cinnamon**
1 tablespoon **caster sugar**

Cinnamon cream
1 tablespoon **icing sugar**
150 ml (¼ pint) **whipping
  cream**
¼ teaspoon **ground
  cinnamon**

Put the cherries in a large bowl. Place the sugar in a heavy-based saucepan and add the measured water, vanilla pod, cloves and orange peel. Bring to the boil, stirring occasionally, then pour the syrup over the cherries. Leave to cool.

Make the crumble. Cut the fruit loaf into 1 cm (½ inch) dice. Melt the butter and drizzle it over the fruit loaf. Mix together the cinnamon and sugar and sprinkle over the fruit loaf. Mix well, transfer to a baking sheet and cook in a preheated oven, 190°C (375°F), Gas Mark 5, for 4–5 minutes until golden and crunchy. Remove the crumble from the oven and allow to cool.

Meanwhile, make the cinnamon cream. Sift the icing sugar over the cream, add the cinnamon and whisk until firm peaks form.

Serve the cherries with a small amount of syrup, a spoonful of the cinnamon cream and a sprinkling of the fruit loaf crumble. Decorate with strips of orange peel.

pink grapefruit cream

Calories per serving **463** (not
 including brandy snaps)
Serves **4**
Preparation time **15 minutes**

2 **pink grapefruits**
5 tablespoons **dark brown
 sugar**, plus extra for
 sprinkling
250 ml (8 fl oz) **double cream**
150 g (5 oz) **Greek yogurt**
3 tablespoons **concentrated
 elderflower cordial**
½ teaspoon **ground ginger**
½ teaspoon **ground
 cinnamon**
brandy snaps, to serve
 (optional)

Grate the rind of 1 grapefruit finely, making sure you
don't take any of the bitter white pith. Cut the skin
and the white membrane off both grapefruits, and cut
between the membranes to remove the segments.
Place in a large dish, sprinkle with 2 tablespoons of the
sugar and set aside.

Whisk the cream in a large bowl until thick but not stiff.
Fold in the yogurt, elderflower cordial, spices, grapefruit
rind and remaining sugar until smooth.

Spoon the mixture into attractive glasses, arranging the
grapefruit segments between layers of grapefruit cream.
Sprinkle the top with a little extra sugar, add the brandy
snaps, if liked, and serve immediately.

For spiced orange cream, finely grate the rind of
2 large oranges, then cut away the pith and membrane
to release the orange segments. Sprinkle with
2 tablespoons of the sugar and set aside. Whip the
cream, then flavour as above, adding the orange rind in
place of the grapefruit rind. **Calories per serving 472**

pear, apple & cinnamon crumble

Calories per serving **465**
Serves **6**
Preparation time **10 minutes**
Cooking time **30–35 minutes**

750 g (1½ lb) **pears**, peeled,
  cored and sliced
500 g (1 lb) **cooking apples**,
  peeled, cored and sliced
2 tablespoons **soft light
  brown sugar**
1 teaspoon **ground cinnamon**
4 tablespoons **apple juice**

Topping
200 g (7 oz) **rice flour**
100 g (3½ oz) **butter**, cubed
100 g (3½ oz) **soft light
  brown sugar**
25 g (1oz) **flaked almonds**
25 g (1 oz) **blanched
  hazelnuts**, roughly chopped

Put the pears and apples in a large saucepan with the sugar, cinnamon and apple juice. Cover and cook gently, stirring occasionally, for about 10 minutes or until the fruit is just tender. Transfer to an ovenproof dish.

Make the topping. Place the flour and butter in a food processor and whizz until the mixture resembles fine breadcrumbs. Alternatively, place the flour in a large bowl, add the butter and rub in with the fingertips until the mixture resembles fine breadcrumbs. Stir in the sugar and nuts, then sprinkle over the fruit and press down gently.

Place in a preheated oven, 200°C (400°F), Gas Mark 6, for 20–25 minutes until golden and bubbling.

For rhubarb & ginger crumble, cut 1 kg (2 lb) rhubarb into chunks and put in an ovenproof dish with 2 tablespoons water and 6 tablespoons caster sugar. Place in a preheated oven, 200°C (400°F), Gas Mark 6, for 15 minutes, then stir in 1 teaspoon ground ginger. Make the topping as above, adding 100 g (3½ oz) finely chopped marzipan. Sprinkle over the rhubarb and bake in the oven as above. **Calories per serving 497**

berry meringue mess

Calories per serving **467**
Serves **6**
Preparation time **10 minutes**
Cooking time **1 hour**

4 **egg whites**
200 g (7 oz) **caster sugar**
1 teaspoon **white wine
vinegar**
285 ml (10 fl oz) **double
cream**
300 g (10 oz) **raspberries**,
plus extra, left whole, to
decorate
250 g (8 oz) **strawberries**,
hulled and quartered,
plus extra, left whole and
unhulled, to decorate
2 tablespoons **icing sugar**
2 tablespoons **cream liqueur**

Line 2 large baking sheets with nonstick baking paper.

Whisk the egg whites in a large clean bowl until they form stiff peaks. Add the sugar a spoonful at a time and continue to whisk until thick and glossy. Fold in the vinegar with a large metal spoon.

Spoon or pipe 12 meringues onto the prepared baking sheets. Place in a preheated oven, 150°C (300°F), Gas Mark 2, for 1 hour, then switch off the oven and leave the meringues inside to cool completely. When cool, roughly crush the meringues.

Whip the cream in a large bowl until it forms soft peaks. Roughly crush together the raspberries and strawberries and stir into the cream. Fold in the crushed meringues, icing sugar and cream liqueur. Spoon into 6 tall glasses, decorate with extra whole berries and serve immediately.

For mango & passion fruit mess, make the meringues as above and roughly crush. Whip the cream with 2 tablespoons icing sugar in a large bowl until it forms soft peaks. Peel and pit 1 large mango and purée half the flesh in a food processor or blender. Chop the remaining mango flesh and stir all the mango into the cream mixture with the scooped flesh of 2 passion fruit. Fold in the crushed meringues and serve immediately.
Calories per serving 475

baked apples & flapjack crumble

Calories per serving **488** (not including ice cream or crème fraîche)
Serves **4**
Preparation time **15 minutes**
Cooking time **20–25 minutes**

4 **dessert apples**, halved and cored
75 g (3 oz) **raisins**
4 tablespoons **golden syrup**
6 tablespoons **apple juice** or **water**
50 g (2 oz) **plain flour**
50 g (2 oz) **rolled oats**
50 g (2 oz) **light muscovado sugar**
50 g (2 oz) **unsalted butter**, at room temperature, diced
2 tablespoons **sunflower seeds**
2 tablespoons **sesame seeds**
vanilla ice cream or **crème fraîche**, to serve (optional)

Arrange the apples, cut side up, in a shallow ovenproof dish. Divide the raisins among the apples, pressing them into the core cavity. Drizzle with 2 tablespoons of the golden syrup and add the apple juice or water to the base of the dish.

Put the flour, oats, sugar and butter into a small bowl and rub in the butter with fingertips until the mixture resembles fine breadcrumbs. Stir in the seeds. Spoon the crumble over the top of the apples and mound up. Drizzle with the remaining syrup.

Cook in a preheated oven, 180°C (350°F), Gas Mark 4, for 20–25 minutes until the crumble is golden and the apples are soft. Serve warm with scoops of vanilla ice cream or crème fraîche, if liked.

For plum & muesli crumble, halve 10 plums and place them, cut side up, in an ovenproof dish. Drizzle with 2 tablespoons honey and add 6 tablespoons red grape juice or water to the base of the dish. Make the crumble, using 75 g (3 oz) of muesli instead of the oats and seeds. Bake and serve as above. **Calories per serving 393**

flourless chocolate cake

Calories per serving **488**
Cuts into **12**
Preparation time **25 minutes**
Cooking time **1 hour**

125 g (4 oz) **blanched almonds**, roughly chopped
125 g (4 oz) **Brazil nuts**, roughly chopped
225 g (7½ oz) **plain dark chocolate**, chopped into 5 mm (¼ inch) pieces
225 g (7½ oz) **slightly salted butter**, softened
4 **eggs**, separated
225 g (7½ oz) **golden caster sugar**
sifted **cocoa powder**, for dusting

Put the almonds, Brazil nuts and chocolate in a food processor and process until the consistency of ground almonds. Beat together the butter, egg yolks and 175 g (6 oz) of the sugar in a bowl until pale and creamy. Stir in the chocolate mixture.

Whisk the egg whites in a large clean bowl with a hand-held electric whisk until peaking. Gradually whisk in the remaining sugar, a spoonful at a time. Stir a quarter of the mixture into the creamed mixture using a large metal spoon. Add the remaining egg whites and stir gently to mix.

Spoon the mixture into a greased and lined 23 cm (9 inch) loose-bottomed or spring-form cake tin and level the surface. Bake in a preheated oven, 160°C (325°F), Gas Mark 3, for about 1 hour or until just firm to the touch and a skewer inserted into the centre comes out clean.

Leave to cool in the tin (the centre of the cake will sink slightly), then remove the ring and base and dust with sifted cocoa powder. Serve with fresh raspberry compote, if liked (see below).

For fresh raspberry compote, to serve as an accompaniment, put 75 g (3 oz) fresh raspberries, 40 g (1½ oz) caster sugar, 1 teaspoon vanilla extract and 1 tablespoon water in a small saucepan. Cook for about 5 minutes until the raspberries are soft and mushy. Strain through a sieve into a bowl and stir in a further 225 g (7½ oz) raspberries. Mix gently until coated in the sauce. Chill until ready to serve. **Calories per serving 21**

autumn fruit oaty crumble

Calories per serving **495**
Serves **4**
Preparation time **15 minutes**
Cooking time **40–45 minutes**

1 **dessert apple**, peeled,
  cored and sliced
25 g (1 oz) ready-to-eat **dried
  apples**, chopped (optional)
400 g (13 oz) can **pear halves**
  in juice, drained and roughly
  chopped, with 4 tablespoons
  juice reserved
200 g (7 oz) **ripe plums**,
  halved, stoned and quartered
25 g (1 oz) **raisins** or **golden
  raisins**
4 tablespoons **fat-free Greek
  yogurt**, to serve (optional)

Topping
75 g (3 oz) **wholemeal flour**
50 g (2 oz) **rolled oats**
25 g (1 oz) **bran**
pinch of **salt**
50 g (2 oz) **pecan nuts**,
  chopped
2 tablespoons **soft dark
  brown sugar**
¾ teaspoon **mixed spice**
75 g (3 oz) **butter**, melted

Put all the prepared fruit and raisins into a shallow,
rectangular ovenproof dish, approximately 28 x 20 cm
(11 x 8 inches). Drizzle over the reserved pear juice.

Mix together the dry topping ingredients in a large
bowl. Pour over the melted butter and combine until the
mixture resembles large breadcrumbs. Sprinkle over the
fruit and press down firmly.

Place in a preheated oven, 180°C (350°F), Gas Mark 4,
for 40–45 minutes or until golden and crisp. Serve with
1 tablespoon fat-free Greek yogurt per person, if liked.

For forest fruit & clementine crumble, replace the
fresh and dried fruits with 450 g (14½ oz) frozen forest
fruits, thawed and drained of excess liquid. Slice 2
clementines into segments, discarding the pith, and mix
with the forest fruits. Spread the fruit over the base of
the ovenproof dish, cover with the crumble topping and
bake as above. Serve with 1 tablespoon fat-free Greek
yogurt per person, if liked. **Calories per serving 438**

index

236

acknowledgements

Commissioning editor: Eleanor Maxfield
Senior editor: Ellie Smith
Editor: Pollyanna Poulter
Designer: Jeremy Tilston
Production controller: Allison Gonsalves

Photography: Octopus Publishing Group Limited 18–19;
Stephen Conroy 6–7, 115, 139, 157, 177, 179, 181, 187;
Will Heap 4–5, 8, 10, 11 left, 12 left, 12 right, 13, 21, 23, 27,
31, 39, 49, 55, 57, 63, 67, 83, 99, 119, 129, 131, 133, 145,
161, 195, 205, 207, 211, 213, 215, 221, 231; David Munns
123, 151, 169; Emma Neish 109; Lis Parsons 11 right, 15,
25, 35, 51, 61, 73, 75, 77, 81, 85, 87, 91, 93, 97, 117, 125,
141, 149, 185, 193, 197, 199, 203, 209, 217, 219, 223,
225; Gareth Sambidge 47, 147, 191; William Shaw 1, 2–3,
9, 29, 33, 37, 41, 43, 45, 53, 59, 65, 69, 78–79, 95, 101,
103, 105, 107, 111, 113, 121, 127, 135, 137, 153, 155,
162–163, 165, 167, 171, 173, 175, 189, 200–201, 227,
229, 233, 235; Ian Wallace 71, 89, 143, 159, 183.